a **WEE** ♥ **UIDE** *to*
Robert the Bruce

Battle of Bannockburn (right panel, mural by William Hole)

a **WEE GUIDE** *to*

Robert the Bruce

Duncan Jones & Alison L. Rae

GOBLINSHEAD

Edinburgh

a **WEE GUIDE** to Robert the Bruce

First Published 1996
Reprinted 1997, 1999, 2002
© Martin Coventry 1996
Text © Duncan Jones, Alison L. Rae, Martin Coventry 1996
Published by GOBLINSHEAD
130B Inveresk Road
Musselburgh EH21 7AY
Scotland
tel 0131 665 2894; *fax* 0131 653 6566
email goblinshead@sol.co.uk

British Library Cataloguing in Publication Data
A catalogue record for this book is available from the British Library.

ISBN 1 899874 02 X

Typeset by GOBLINSHEAD using Desktop Publishing
Typeset in Garamond Narrow

WEE GUIDES
William Wallace
The Picts
Scottish History
The Jacobites
Robert Burns
Mary, Queen of Scots
Robert the Bruce
Haunted Castles of Scotland
Old Churches and Abbeys of Scotland
Castles and Mansions of Scotland
New for 1999
Prehistoric Scotland
Macbeth and Early Scotland
Whisky

a **WEE GUIDE** *to*
Robert the Bruce

Contents

List of maps

List of illustrations

Acknowledgements

The illustrations on the following pages are reproduced by kind permission: Statue of Robert the Bruce at Bannockburn (cover and page 86) National Trust for Scotland, Edinburgh; Battle of Bannockburn, right panel, mural by William Hole (frontispage) The Scottish National Portrait Gallery; Declaration of Arbroath (pages 59 & 80) Scottish Record Office, Edinburgh; Brass Marking Robert the Bruce's Tomb (page 67) Tim Tiley Ltd, Bristol; Reconstruction of Robert the Bruce's head (page 69) Forensic sculpting by Brian Hill AIMI ARPS RMIP, Head of Department of Medical Illustration, The Dental Hospital, Newcastle upon Tyne, commissioned by the National Galleries of Scotland, Edinburgh.

Crowning of Robert the Bruce (page 22), Capture of Edinburgh Castle (page 39), and Bruce and de Bohun (page 45) by Catriona Campbell; Stirling Castle (page 11), Urquhart Castle (page 31) and Bothwell Castle (page 50) by Laura Ferguson. Family trees (page 9 & 21) and battle plans of Bannockburn (pages 43 & 47-9) by Duncan Jones; maps and photographs by Martin Coventry.

How to use this book

This book is divided into two sections:

- The text (pages 2–69) describes Robert the Bruce's life and the events surrounding him, with maps (pages 4, 24, 52 & 54). Family trees illustrate the relationship of Robert to the kings of Scots, and to his own family (pages 9 & 21). A calendar of events summarises the period chronologically (page 2). Four battle plans cover the sequence of events at Bannockburn (pages 43 & 47-9).

- Places, associated with Robert the Bruce, to visit (pages 70-79) listing over 30 castles and abbeys in Scotland and England, as well as the Battle of Bannockburn battlefield (page 71). Information includes access, opening, facilities, and a brief description; and a map locates all the sites in Scotland (page 70).

Two appendices conclude the book. Appendix I contains the full text of the Declaration of Arbroath (page 80), while Appendix II looks at Robert the Bruce's life and times as king, patriot and man (page 84).

Illustrations of particular interest include a model of Bruce's head reconstructed from his skull (page 69), and the brass marking his tomb at Dunfermline (page 67).

An index (pages 87-8) lists all the main people, battles and events.

Warning

While the information in this book was believed to be correct at time of going to press – and was checked, where possible, with the visitor attractions – opening times and facilities, or other information, may vary or differ from that included. All information should be checked with the visitor attractions before embarking on any journey. Inclusion in the text is no indication whatsoever that a site is open to the public or that it should be visited. Many sites, particularly ruined castles and churches, are potentially dangerous and great care should be taken: the publisher and author cannot accept responsibility for damage or injury caused from any visit.

The places listed to visit are only a personal selection of what is available in Scotland, and the inclusion or exclusion of a visitor attraction in the text should not be considered as a comment or judgement on that attraction.

Locations, boundaries and territories on maps may be approximate.

Introduction

Robert the Bruce is one of Scotland's most famous kings and heroes, and yet, apart from 'beating the English at Bannockburn', most people know very little about his story. We have tried to give a brief outline of him here: the man, his times and the struggle for Scottish independence. Although this account is concise, we have included every major event. Also covered are several episodes of lesser importance – such as the gruesome fate of the treacherous blacksmith of Kildrummy, or the dangerous cattle of Roxburgh – because we liked the stories.

Various individuals are quoted throughout the text. These quotations are drawn from original sources such as the Chronicle of Lanercost or the epic 14th-century poem *The Brus* by John Barbour. Obviously, these are not verbatim records of the precise words spoken, but the sense is the same. They can also help to show how these people were seen by their contemporaries.

Many people today see Robert Bruce as an opportunistic adventurer, looking after his own best interests. In Appendix II we try to address this issue, and give a short overview of his career and motivation. You can decide for yourself if you agree.

Finally, we would like to thank friends and family for all their help and encouragement. Special thanks go to Catriona Campbell for her illustrations.

DJ & ALR, Glasgow, November 1996

Calendar of events

1274   Birth of Robert Bruce.

1286   Death of Alexander III. Election of Guardians.

1289   Treaty of Salisbury.

1290   Treaty of Birgham. Death of Maid of Norway.

1291   Edward I accepted as superior lord of Scotland. Court of claims opened.

1292   Balliol crowned.

1294   War between England and France. Welsh revolt.

1295   Council of Twelve replaces King John. Treaty between France and Scotland. Robert Bruce the Competitor dies.

1296   War between England and Scotland. Sack of Berwick. Battle of Dunbar. King John abdicates. Edward I receives homage at Berwick Parliament.

1297   Uprising under Andrew Murray and William Wallace. Robert Bruce joins with Scots. Capitulation at Irvine. Battle of Stirling Bridge. William Lamberton appointed Bishop of St Andrews. Andrew Murray dies.

1298   Wallace knighted and appointed sole Guardian. Edward I invades Scotland. Battle of Falkirk. Bruce and John Comyn appointed Guardians.

1299   Bishop Lamberton appointed third Guardian. Scots take Stirling Castle.

1300   Bruce resigns Guardianship, replaced by Ingram de Umfraville. English invasion. Truce.

1301   John Soulis appointed sole Guardian. English invasion.

1302   Truce. Bruce submits to Edward I and marries Elizabeth de Burgh.

1303   Battle of Roslin. Treaty between England and France. Edward I invades Scotland for the last time.

1304   Scots submit to Edward I. Bruce's father dies. Edward I captures Stirling. Bond between Bruce and Lamberton.

1305   Wallace captured and executed.

1306   Bruce murders Comyn at Dumfries. Bruce crowned King of Scots. Battle of Methven. Battle of Dalry. Bruce flees to Rathlin. Nigel Bruce captured and executed. Bruce women imprisoned.

1307   Alexander and Thomas Bruce captured and executed. Bruce lands at Turnberry. Ambush at Glen Trool. Battle of Loudon Hill. Edward I dies.

1308 Battle of Inverurie. Battle of Brander. Earl of Ross submits to Bruce.

1309 St Andrews parliament.

1310 Edward II's expedition in Scotland.

1311 Bruce raids northern England.

1312 Treaty of Inverness between Norway and Scotland.

1313 Bruce captures Perth, south-west Scotland and the Isle of Man.

1314 Douglas captures Roxburgh. Randolph captures Edinburgh. Battle of Bannockburn. Cambuskenneth parliament.

1315 Succession settled on Edward Bruce. Edward Bruce invades Ireland.

1316 Edward Bruce crowned King of Ireland. Marjorie Bruce dies. Birth of Robert Stewart.

1317 Edward and Robert Bruce make royal progress round Ireland.

1318 Capture of Berwick. Edward Bruce killed in Ireland. Succession settled on Robert Stewart.

1319 Edward II besieges Berwick. Douglas and Randolph invade England. Two-year truce.

1320 Declaration of Arbroath. Soulis conspiracy.

1322 Edward II's last invasion of Scotland. Bruce raids England. Battle of Old Byland.

1323 Bruce-Harclay treaty. 13-year truce.

1324 Pope recognises Bruce as King of Scots. Birth of David Bruce.

1326 Treaty of Corbeil between France and Scotland. Succession to throne settled on David Bruce.

1327 Edward II deposed. Scots attack Norham. Edward III outwitted by Douglas and Randolph at Stanhope Park. Bruce invades Northumberland. Queen Elizabeth dies.

1328 Treaty of Edinburgh. David Bruce marries Edward III's sister Joan.

1329 Robert Bruce dies, 7 June. David II crowned King of Scots.

1330 James Douglas dies.

1332 Thomas Randolph dies.

Map 1: 1286–1306 (Chapters 1–4)

Ross

Elgin

Buchan

Strathbogie

Inverness

Moray

Badenoch

Mar

Aberdeen

SCOTLAND

Mearns

Atholl

Montrose

Angus

Scone

Dundee

Perth

St Andrews

Argyll

Strathearn

Fife

Menteith

Stirling ✗(1297)

Dumbarton

Falkirk
(1298) ✗

Dunfermline

Kinghorn

Dunbar
(1296) ✗

Lennox

Leith

Glasgow

Kirkliston

Edinburgh

Bothwell

Lothian

Berwick

Kyle

Lanark

Peebles

Norham

Irvine

Wark

Douglas

Roxburgh

Selkirk

Ayr

Jedburgh

Turnberry

Carrick

Northumberland

Dalswinton

Lochmaben

ENGLAND

Dumfries

Galloway

Caerlaverock

Carlisle

Cumberland

1–Scotland in Crisis

On the stormy night of 18 March 1286, Alexander III, King of Scots, travelled from Edinburgh Castle to join his new French bride at the royal manor of Kinghorn. Against all advice to wait until the storm and night had passed, he took a ferry across the Firth of Forth and set off along the cliff tops. But in the dark his guides lost touch with him, and in the morning the King was found dead on the shore, his neck broken. Scotland was plunged into a dynastic crisis which would not be resolved fully for another 40 years.

Scotland was a small kingdom, linked by trade and by royal and noble marriage to Norway, England, Flanders and France, among others. The south and east were ruled by nobles and knights, who held their lands from the king and paid their rent in military service. The north and west were still dominated by the Celtic clans, who often disregarded the king in the Lowlands and largely went their own way.

The landscape was very different from what we see today. Instead of great open stretches of fields, much of the countryside was woodland, marsh or moor, with small fields clustered around towns and villages like islands in a sea of wilderness. Rivers and lochs were generally broader and deeper, and there were some then in existence that have left no trace. North of the Forth, the great Caledonian Forest still remained. The Highlands were densely forested, and wolves and boar still roamed there. Roads were few and often little more than simple trackways.

Of course, not all of Scotland was wild. There were many towns, where the mercantile, commercial and administrative activities of the kingdom took place. The most successful towns had grown up at important places, such as Stirling, the *gateway to the north*, with its bridge across the Forth; Edinburgh, with its strong fortress and nearby port of Leith; Berwick, Scotland's principal trading port; and St Andrews, a major ecclesiastical centre and place of pilgrimage. The Church was an important institution in the Middle Ages. The Scottish bishops were fiercely protective of their independence from the richer and more powerful English bishops to the south, and the Scottish Church was to play an important part in Scotland's fight for freedom from English domination.

Alexander III had outlived his first wife and all his children. The only direct heir to the Scottish throne was his infant granddaughter Margaret, the Maid of Norway. Forty days after the tragedy, when it was confirmed

5

that the King's widow was not pregnant, the magnates of the realm – bishops, abbots and priors, earls and barons – gathered at Scone to swear loyalty to the three-year-old Queen in Norway. They elected six Guardians who formed a provisional government to represent the community of the realm of Scotland. Two of the country's leading nobles, Robert Bruce, Lord of Annandale and grandfather of the future King, and John Balliol of Galloway, harboured their own claims to the throne. Neither was appointed as a Guardian, but each had three Guardians who supported them.

For much of Alexander III's reign, relations with England had been generally cordial. The Scone parliament sent three envoys to Gascony to find Edward I, King of England, to inform him of the situation and to ask for his advice and protection.

By 1289, only four of the Guardians remained. Seeing an opportunity of gaining power over Scotland, Edward I asked for and received a papal bull permitting the marriage of Margaret of Norway to his infant son, Edward of Caernarvon, despite the two children being second cousins. The Scots signed a treaty at Birgham in 1290, agreeing to the marriage and to the creation of a union of Scotland and England, while preserving Scotland's independence. Edward I's true intent was revealed by his appointment – before any wedding – of a lieutenant in Scotland, the Bishop of Durham; and in June an English force seized the strategically important Isle of Man.

In September 1290 the young Margaret set sail from Norway to Orkney, then a territory of Norway, but during the voyage she fell ill. She died upon reaching Orkney, leaving the succession to the Scottish throne wide open and the realm in crisis once more.

On hearing the news of the Maid's death, Robert Bruce of Annandale immediately gathered together a strong force and John Balliol, now Lord of Galloway, declared himself *heir to Scotland*. Perceiving the threat of civil war, one of the Guardians, William Fraser, Bishop of St Andrews, wrote to Edward I, urging him to help decide the succession and prevent bloodshed.

Edward I invited the Scottish magnates and various claimants to the throne to Norham in May 1291. He declared that he would resolve their dispute, but not until they recognised him as supreme overlord of Scotland. After several weeks the representatives replied that they could not answer for any future king, but eventually all the claimants, eager for a decision, agreed to Edward's demands. Their decision may have been

Norham Castle

aided by the imminent arrival of an English army at the Border.

In June, the Guardians and magnates handed over custody of the country and royal castles to Edward, with his promise to restore them to the rightful king within two months of his judgement. Many important Scots came to Norham to pay homage. In August Edward established a court at Berwick which, for the next 18 months, heard the claims of all the competitors. The court was made up of 104 arbiters: 24 nominated by Edward I, 40 nominated by Robert Bruce, and 40 nominated by John Balliol – clearly acknowledging the two principal claims from the outset. A total of 13 competitors lodged claims, but many were remote and were made as a formality. Six claimed through illegitimate descendants of William the Lyon – and were ruled out. Only four claimants were taken seriously: John Balliol, Lord of Galloway; Robert Bruce, Lord of Annandale; John Hastings of Abergavenny; and Florence V, Count of Holland. All four were direct descendants of Henry, son of David I: the first three through his youngest son David, Earl of Huntingdon, and the fourth through his daughter Ada.

The Count of Holland claimed that the Earl of Huntingdon had resigned all claim to the throne in return for lands, but he was unable to produce any evidence of this. John Hastings claimed that the kingdom should be divided between the heirs of David of Huntingdon's three daughters, but the first decision of the court was that the kingdom should remain intact. John Balliol claimed through the senior line. Robert Bruce claimed by nearness of degree: he was a grandson of David of Huntingdon; John Balliol was a great-grandson.

In November 1292, Robert Bruce the Competitor learned that his claim would not be successful. Before the decision was announced, he resigned his claim to the throne to his son, the Earl of Carrick, also Robert Bruce. He in turn promptly resigned his Earldom to his own son, also Robert Bruce, future King of Scots.

On 17 November 1292, the King of England's judgement in favour of John Balliol was announced. King John was enthroned at Scone on St Andrew's Day – 30 November – 1292, and subsequently paid homage to Edward I as his superior lord.

Edward I was quick to display his full authority as supreme lord of Scotland, and within a week of John's enthronement he began to hear appeals from the Scottish court in his own court. A number of Scottish magnates protested that Edward should uphold the treaties which respected the laws and customs of Scotland. Edward then renounced all promises made during the vacancy of the throne, and King John was persuaded to declare the Treaty of Birgham null and void.

In May 1294 Edward I declared war on France. He called upon the Scottish king, earls and barons for military service, but they refused. He also called upon the Welsh, confidently distributing arms among them. As Edward prepared to sail for Gascony in September, a rebellion broke out across Wales. The English King was forced to stay and deal with the revolt, which lasted until the following March. In the meantime, the Scottish magnates had decided to fight for Scotland's independence. At Stirling in July 1295, having lost faith in Balliol, they elected a council of twelve to govern the country. Although he was still King, Balliol was declared *incompetent* to rule, as if he were a child. This unprecedented move showed the strength of Scottish desire for an independent kingdom. By October the council had negotiated a defensive alliance with France, ratified in February 1296, effectively declaring war on England.

The Scottish council issued a call to arms at Caddonlee, near Selkirk, for 11 March, as Edward I summoned his army to Newcastle. The Scottish fight for independence was about to begin.

The Scottish Royal Succession

(bold type indicates claimants to the throne, 1291–1292)

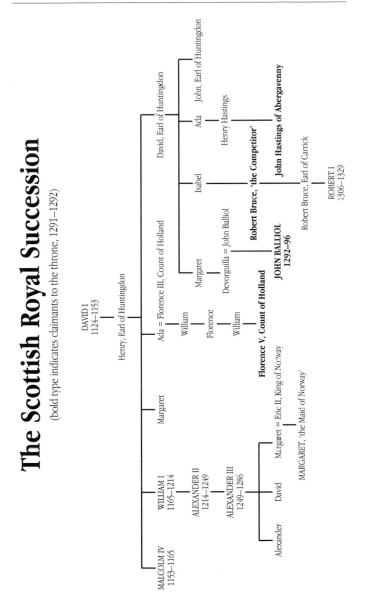

2–The Fight for Independence

The conflict began when an Englishman, Robert de Ros, Lord of Wark-on-Tweed, expressed his intent to marry a Scots girl by joining forces with the Scots and promising his castle to them. His brother requested Edward I's help, but the English guard sent to the castle were ambushed and killed in their camp by de Ros and men from Roxburgh.

When Edward heard the news he exclaimed, *By God's blessing, as the Scots have begun, so shall I make an end.* After Easter, Edward began his advance up the eastern route at Berwick. The Scots ravaged south of the Border and tried to take Carlisle, but were repelled by the Lord of Annandale and the Earl of Carrick. Opposed to Balliol, the Bruces remained loyal to Edward I.

Facing no opposition, Edward's army assaulted Berwick on 30 March. He gave orders that no life should be spared: a massacre ensued for two days, and only ended when the King himself was repulsed to witness a woman put to the sword during childbirth. The governor, Sir William Douglas, surrendered as a hostage to guarantee the safety of the castle garrison. Berwick, once the centre of Scotland's commerce, became the headquarters of Edward's Scottish administration.

The Scots retaliated by raiding throughout Northumberland, burning churches and villages: one record described the burning alive of 200 boys in their school in Corbridge. Their raiding was useless, for it did not distract the English King from his purpose.

Edward marched north to Dunbar. The Countess of Dunbar had handed the castle to the Scots in her husband's absence. On 23 April, English cavalry under John de Warenne, Earl of Surrey, was sent to besiege the castle. After four days, they were attacked by the Scots, under the Earl of Buchan, from the nearby hills. At the sight of their army, the Scots in the castle cheered and raised their banners, taunting the English besiegers with the cry, *Tailed dogs, we will cut your tails off!* – it was a popular joke across Medieval Europe that the English had tails.

Leaving a force to prevent the castle garrison from joining the main Scottish army, Warenne led his knights out to meet the attackers. At one point they rode down into a valley and out of sight. The Scots believed their enemy was fleeing and broke ranks to pursue them. But the English were well-ordered and ready to attack: they fell upon the disordered Scots and overwhelmed them at the first encounter. The Scots fled back across the hills, but thousands of foot soldiers were slaughtered and many of the Scottish nobles were captured.

Edward's progress north was merely a formality. The castles of Roxburgh, Jedburgh and Edinburgh quickly surrendered, and Stirling was

Stirling Castle

found abandoned – only the porter remained to hand over the keys. In Perth, at Midsummer, Edward received letters of submission from King John. On 8 July, Balliol surrendered at Montrose. Edward demanded that he resign his kingdom, renounce the French treaty, and his seal be broken. Balliol was humiliated by having his royal crest ripped from his jacket and thrown on the floor. He was later nicknamed Toom Tabard – *Empty Jacket* or *King Nobody*. He was escorted to the Tower of London, then to Hertfordshire, until he was released into the custody of the Pope in 1299. In the summer of 1301 he was released and allowed to live in freedom on his lands in France for his remaining years.

Edward had gone as far north as Elgin by late July 1296 before returning south. As symbols of his conquest he plundered the Stone of Destiny from Scone and the royal regalia – including the *Black Rood* of St Margaret, Scotland's holiest relic. These treasures were sent to Westminster Abbey. The conqueror returned to Berwick and on 28 August held a parliament, organising his new Scottish administration and receiving oaths of fealty from over 2000 Scots. Their names were recorded in the *Ragman Roll*.

The government of
Scotland was assigned to
Englishmen: John de
Warenne was made
viceroy; Hugh
Cressingham, treasurer;
Sir Walter of Amersham,
chancellor; and Sir William
Ormesby, chief justice.
Scottish nobles were
either imprisoned in
England or paid
homage to Edward.

Throughout the war the
Bruce family had stayed
on good terms with
Edward, having never
recognised John Balliol as
king. They were further
encouraged by Edward's

The Stone of Destiny beneath the Coronation Chair. The Stone was returned to Scotland in 1996.

promise that should the revolt be crushed and Balliol deposed, the Lord
of Annandale would succeed to the Scottish throne. After Dunbar, the
Lord of Annandale reminded the English King of his promise. Edward
denied the throne to the Bruces once again, with the rebuke, *Have we
nothing else to do but win kingdoms for you?* As far as the English King
was concerned, Scotland had ceased to exist as a separate kingdom. Now
it was merely part of a greater England.

Returning south to resume his war with France, Edward believed the
Scots had been crushed. Warenne despised Scotland and returned to his
estates in Yorkshire, leaving Cressingham to raise taxes from the Scots to
help fund the war against France. Those who did not proclaim fealty to
Edward were outlawed and their property and possessions seized.
Cressingham soon became hated by the Scots – they nicknamed him the
treacherer.

Opposition gradually re-emerged in Scotland. Two of the original
Guardians of 1286 remained in the country – Robert Wishart, Bishop of
Glasgow, and James Stewart – and they organised much of the
resistance. Bands of men began to gather in the forests and hills, and two

prominent leaders emerged. In the north, Andrew Murray, a noble who had been captured at Dunbar but had escaped; in the south, William Wallace, son of a knightly family who had refused to swear oaths of fealty to Edward and was outlawed.

Increasing numbers of men flocked to join them, including Sir William Douglas, the former governor of Berwick. Encouraged by this example, some nobles made shows of strength. In July, James Stewart and Bishop Wishart assembled with other nobles at Irvine. It was now that they were joined by the young Robert Bruce, Earl of Carrick.

Edward I was preoccupied with the French conflict. He had instructed the Governor of Carlisle to send his son, Robert Bruce, now 22 years old, with the men of Annandale to capture the castle of Sir William Douglas, held by Douglas's wife. When Bruce reached the castle he did not attack, but instead turned to his men and said, *No man holds his flesh and blood in hatred and I am no exception. I must join my own people and the nation in which I was born. Choose then whether you go with me or return to your homes.*

Balliol had been deposed: the rebellion was now led by the same men that had supported his grandfather's claim to the throne. Edward I, not John Balliol, was now the enemy. Bruce headed north with many of his men, the men of Douglas and other recruits, to join the other leaders at Irvine.

Alerted to the size of opposition gathering at Irvine, two English barons, Henry Percy and Robert Clifford, led a powerful force to deal with the insurrection. By the end of June they had reached Ayr, but there was no battle. The Scots had a vastly inferior force, mostly of foot soldiers, and they only engaged the English in negotiations for surrender. Bishop Wishart and Sir William Douglas were imprisoned, but Robert Bruce and James Stewart refused to surrender and forfeited their lands. Bruce's father was relieved of his governorship and retired to his estates in England, where he remained until his death in 1304. The deliberately lengthy negotiations allowed Wallace the freedom to continue the revolt. Andrew Murray enjoyed similar success, and by August he had gained control of all the English-held castles in the north.

3—Stirling Bridge and Falkirk

Despite the alarming reports reaching him from Cressingham that almost all of Scotland north of the Forth was in the hands of the Scots, Edward I sailed for Flanders, determined to pursue the campaign against France.

Warenne gathered an army of heavy cavalry and infantry at Berwick and marched towards Stirling, the *gateway to the north*. By now Wallace and Murray had joined forces, and as Warenne and Cressingham approached Stirling from the south, the Scots massed at the Abbey Craig, a mile north of the single bridge across the Forth. Between them and the Forth ran a causeway, surrounded by marshy ground. Their army, made up almost entirely of footsoldiers, was greatly outnumbered by the English.

The English arrived confident of an easy victory, and were met by Scottish lords who offered to negotiate with Wallace and Murray. But they could not persuade their countrymen to withdraw. On the morning of 11 September, the English army began crossing the narrow bridge two abreast. When sufficient of the column had crossed, Wallace and Murray attacked with their spearmen. They split their army in two, to attack the leading ranks and to seize the north end of the bridge. They hacked away at the timbers of the bridge until it collapsed, plunging horses and riders into the river below. Driven off the causeway, the English knights

Stirling Old Bridge, dating from the 15th c. – the battle took place near here.

floundered in the boggy ground. The rest of the English army could only watch the ensuing bloody massacre from the southern bank.

Stirling Bridge was a resounding victory for the Scots. Cressingham was killed – the hated *treacherer* was flayed and small pieces of his skin were sent throughout the country as tokens of liberation. Only one

English knight, Sir Marmaduke Tweng, escaped the bloodshed to find refuge at Stirling Castle. Warenne abandoned the attack and fled with such haste to Berwick that upon arrival his horse collapsed.

William Wallace and Andrew Murray were now entrusted with the Guardianship of Scotland, but Murray had been badly wounded and by November was dead. Nobles who had until now stayed quiet openly declared resistance to the English, notably the Comyns in the north-east and Robert Bruce in the south-west, where he had stayed on his Carrick lands since the events at Irvine.

Soon the English held only a handful of Scottish castles. Throughout the winter, Wallace led raids into Northumberland and Cumberland. During this time, Bishop Fraser of St Andrews died in France and was replaced by William Lamberton, a friend of Bishop Wishart. Lamberton was also to play a major part in the fight for Scotland's independence. The Scottish magnates gathered at a parliament in the Selkirk forest in March 1298, where William Wallace was knighted, probably by Bruce himself.

In January 1298, Philip IV of France signed a truce with Edward I, abandoning the alliance with the Scots. Edward returned to England in March and immediately turned north, transferring his government from London to York. He was determined to crush Scotland, and vowed that the words *Malleus Scottorum* – Hammer of the Scots – would be engraved on his tomb.

Edward summoned a formidable army to Roxburgh in late June, comprising a vast 2000 heavy cavalry and 12 000 foot, mostly Welsh. Early in July they set off on the road to Edinburgh. They found the land deserted of both people and livestock: the inhabitants had fled, driving their cattle and sheep before them.

By 15 July the English army had reached Kirkliston, but it was faced with starvation, drunken brawling and the Welsh threat to join with the Scots. With no knowledge of Wallace's whereabouts, the expedition was near collapse. Only when Edward had decided to return to Edinburgh did his fleet of supplies arrive at Leith. Then a message reached him that the Scots were camped in Callendar Wood near Falkirk, only 13 miles away. Locating the Scots united Edward's army again, and they immediately marched towards the Scottish position. As at Stirling Bridge, the English possessed an overwhelming advantage in heavy cavalry; but here, there was no bridge or causeway to restrict their movements. Wallace could have retreated, but his troops were confident and impatient for battle.

Recognising that they would remain and fight with or without him, Wallace made the best preparations he could.

He chose a strong defensive position, protected at the front by a marsh, on his left by a steep valley, and on his right by broken ground. He formed his men into schiltrons, closely-packed circles of 1000–2000 men, armed with 12-foot-long spears. With the long spears planted firmly on the ground, their iron tips fanning up and outwards, these hedgehog-like formations presented a formidable barrier to charging horsemen. Between the schiltrons were the archers of Ettrick Forest, although their short bows were no match for the range and power of the Welsh longbows. What little cavalry the Scots could muster was positioned on the crest of the hill behind.

The English cavalry charged almost immediately, sending Wallace's cavalry into flight and scattering the Ettrick archers. But the Scottish schiltrons remained firm: again and again the knights charged, but could make no progress. Edward ordered the Welsh longbowmen to unleash a deadly rain of arrows. With men falling all around, the schiltrons began to fragment. The English knights charged again, and broke them apart. Thousands of Scots were slaughtered. Wallace himself barely escaped with his life, fleeing with a handful of men into the surrounding woodland.

Despite this victory, Edward was unable to achieve any further breakthrough. His supplies were low and he could not pursue the remnants of the Scottish army. Returning southwards, he attempted to capture Bruce in Ayr, but found only a deserted town and burnt-out castle. Unable to keep his own army together, Edward returned to Carlisle on 8 September.

4–A King of Scots

Falkirk marked the end of Wallace's 10-month Guardianship, and his subsequent movements are little known: he soon left the country and travelled to the French court. Two new Guardians were appointed towards the end of 1298: Robert Bruce and John Comyn *the Red* of Badenoch, a kinsman of John Balliol. Scotland was still in revolt, despite the defeat at Falkirk, for the English did not have enough troops for an occupation, effectively controlling only east Lothian.

By August 1299, the already uneasy relations between Bruce and Comyn had begun to break down. During a council at Peebles, a quarrel erupted: John Comyn seized Robert Bruce by the throat amidst accusations of treason, and the two men had to be separated. Bishop Lamberton, regarded as a neutral, was appointed principal Guardian. For the time being the feud was patched up.

In November the Scots offered the English King a truce, but he declined. Edward was unable to assemble an army, and by the end of 1299 the starving English garrison of Stirling had surrendered.

By May 1300 Robert Bruce had resigned his Guardianship. The Comyn faction had decided that their efforts should be concentrated in the south-west, where many of Bruce's father's men were still loyal to Edward I, and the men of Galloway were a law unto themselves. Bruce returned to his Carrick lands, and he remained there for the next two years. He was replaced as Guardian by Sir Ingram de Umfraville, a Comyn ally.

Edward I succeeded in raising a sizeable army, and he began his summer campaign by besieging Caerlaverock Castle. The Scottish

Caerlaverock Castle (1910?)

garrison asked for surrender terms, but Edward completed the assault and executed many of the defenders. This, however, was his only success, despite a number of skirmishes with the Scots, led by the Comyns.

As a result of much diplomacy by Bishop Lamberton at the Vatican, Edward received a Papal Bull demanding he withdraw from Scotland. Outraged by this – but under pressure from Philip of France – he agreed a truce from October 1300 until May 1301. He also released Bishop Wishart from prison.

Early in 1301 all three Guardians, unable to cooperate, resigned. Sir John Soulis replaced them as sole Guardian. The Scots sent a diplomatic mission to the Papal court in Rome; English envoys were already there pleading the English case.

The truce ended in May 1301, and attempts to negotiate further peace failed. Edward mounted a campaign into Galloway in July, sending his son Edward up the west coast from Carlisle, while he himself led the main army from Berwick in the east. Again they achieved little, capturing only Selkirk, Peebles, Bothwell and Turnberry. Both forces were constantly harried by Sir John Soulis.

In January 1302 the English King was again pressurised by Philip of France into signing a nine-month truce with the Scots. A rumour spread throughout Scotland that John Balliol would soon be restored to the throne by a French army.

The possibility of Balliol's return threatened Bruce's lands and claim to the throne, and led him to change sides in February, and make his peace with Edward. By his submission, his lands were secured, and he was now able to marry his second wife, Elizabeth de Burgh, daughter of the Earl of Ulster – one of Edward's senior lords in Ireland.

As well as the loss of Bruce and his army, the Scots suffered from political changes in Europe. The French army was defeated by the Flemish at Courtrai in July 1302, and the French King's changing fortune and an escalating quarrel with the Pope led him to seek a truce with England. The Scots urgently sent a delegation to Paris. One of the envoys was John Soulis, and in his absence John Comyn was reinstated as Guardian.

The temporary truce between the Scots and English expired in November 1302. In May 1303 the French and English sealed an alliance, and a provision was made for a marriage between the Prince of Wales and Isabella, the King of France's daughter. Despite their diplomacy in Paris, the Scots were excluded from this peace.

In the same month, Edward I invaded Scotland again. His well-prepared campaign was simply a military parade, beginning in Roxburgh and arriving at Elgin in September, encountering barely any opposition along the way. He then returned south to spend the winter at Dunfermline Abbey. Resistance had fallen apart. In February 1304, John Comyn and other Scottish leaders – though not John Soulis – submitted to Edward. Comyn achieved more reasonable terms of surrender than John Balliol had in 1296, possibly due to Robert Bruce's influence with the English King.

Sir William Oliphant, commander of Stirling Castle, did not accept this surrender. Edward scornfully denied Oliphant's request to seek instructions from John Soulis, and subjected the garrison to a three-

Stirling Castle (1903)

month-long siege, during which he tested every siege engine that he could find. Even when the defenders offered surrender in July, Edward persisted for several more days, and the surrendering garrison was treated very cruelly.

As part of the Scottish submission, Edward had demanded that Sir William Wallace be given up to the English. Wallace was pursued relentlessly until his capture near Glasgow in August 1305. He was taken to London with his legs tied beneath his horse. On 23 August a procession led him to Westminster Hall, where he was tried for his crimes against the English, which he admitted. He was also charged with treason, which he denied, having never sworn homage to Edward as his king. But the trial was a formality, and the judgement a foregone conclusion.

Wallace was dragged behind a horse to the Smithfield Elms, where he was hanged, cut down, disembowelled and beheaded. His heart and entrails were burned, and his body was quartered, the four parts being sent to Newcastle, Berwick, Stirling and Perth. His head was displayed above London Bridge.

In pursuing a personal vendetta and trying to make an example of William Wallace, Edward only succeeded in creating a martyr. Having smashed the Scots, he now expected them to be subdued, but he could not have anticipated events yet to come.

In the summer of June 1304, Robert Bruce and Bishop Lamberton had made a secret pact and had been discussing another revolt. Edward I was old and frequently ill, and was sure to die soon. Upon Edward's death, Bruce planned to claim the Scottish throne and lead the rebellion – the Prince of Wales posed little threat. Bruce's main opposition would come from John Comyn: he had led previous uprisings, however ineffectively, and was still loyal to John Balliol.

In February 1306, Edward's justices were attending a session at Dumfries Castle. Bruce was at Lochmaben, with Comyn nearby at Dalswinton, and Bruce requested a meeting. They met on 10 February at the Greyfriars Church, and at the high altar Bruce offered Comyn lands in return for his help in becoming king. Comyn refused and tempers flared: Bruce stabbed Comyn with his dagger, then Bruce's companions attacked him with their swords. Comyn was left for dead in front of the altar.

Although Comyn's murder was probably unpremeditated, the rebellion had been carefully planned and was now put in motion. Bruce and his supporters quickly seized the castle, then set about gaining control of the south-west.

Bruce then went to Glasgow to join Bishop Wishart, who absolved him of his crime, and the Scottish Church rallied behind Bruce and his cause. A formal notice was sent to Edward I that he should recognise Robert Bruce as King of Scots, and the kingdom was placed on 24-hours notice of mobilisation to arms.

On 25 March 1306 – New Year's Day in the old calendar – in the Abbey of Scone, Robert Bruce was crowned Robert I, King of Scots. Present at the ceremony were the Bishops of Glasgow, St Andrews and Moray, and the Earls of Atholl, Lennox, Menteith and Mar. Bruce wore the kingly robes and vestments which had been kept safe in Bishop Wishart's treasury, and a circlet of gold was placed on his head. This was the traditional privilege of the Earl of Fife, but he was still a minor and a ward of the English King. His aunt Isabel, Countess of Buchan – despite being

The Bruce Family

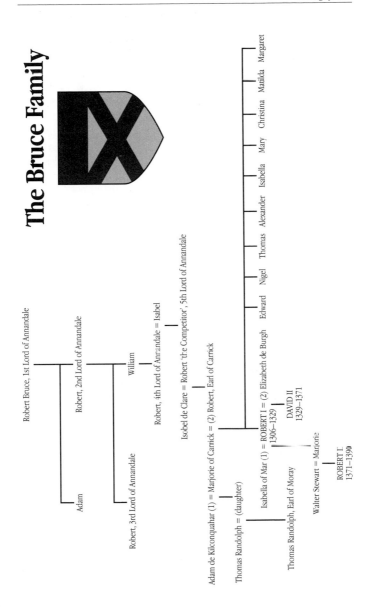

Robert Bruce, 1st Lord of Annandale

Robert, 2nd Lord of Annandale

Adam

William

Robert, 3rd Lord of Annandale

Robert, 4th Lord of Annandale = Isabel

Isobel de Clare = Robert 'the Competitor', 5th Lord of Annandale

Adam de Kilconquhar (1) = Marjorie of Carrick = (2) Robert, Earl of Carrick

Thomas Randolph = (daughter)

Isabella of Mar (1) = ROBERT I = (2) Elizabeth de Burgh
1306–1329

Thomas Randolph, Earl of Moray

DAVID II
1329–1371

Walter Stewart = Marjorie

Edward   Nigel   Thomas   Alexander   Isabella   Mary   Christina   Matilda   Margaret

ROBERT I
1371–1390

Crowning of Robert the Bruce – Robert I, King of Scots (Catriona Campbell)

Scone Palace, built on the site of the Abbey where Robert the Bruce was crowned in 1306.

married to the Earl of Buchan, a Comyn – hastened to Scone to take her nephew's place. A second ceremony was held two days after the first, on Palm Sunday, when the Bishop of St Andrews celebrated High Mass and the gold circlet was once again placed on the King's head.

23

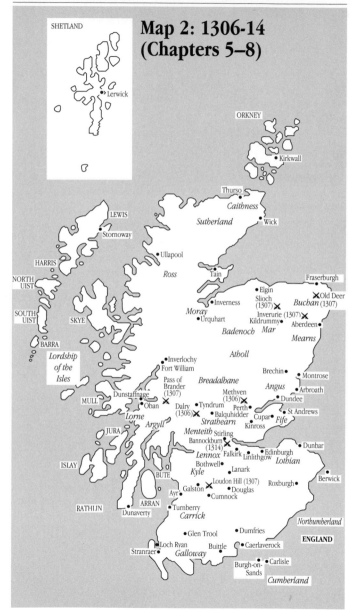

SHETLAND

Lerwick

Map 2: 1306-14
(Chapters 5–8)

ORKNEY

Kirkwall

Thurso
Caithness
Sutherland
Wick

LEWIS

Stornoway

Ullapool

HARRIS

NORTH
UIST
Ross
Tain
Fraserburgh

SOUTH
UIST
SKYE
Elgin
Slioch
(1307) ✕
✕Old Deer
Buchan (1307)

Moray
Inverness
Inverurie (1307)✕
Aberdeen

BARRA
Urquhart
Kildrummy

*Lordship
of the
Isles*
Badenoch
Mar

Atholl
Mearns

Inverlochy
Fort William
Brechin
Montrose

Breadalbane
Pass of
Brander
(1307)
Methven
(1306)✕
Angus
Arbroath

MULL
Dunstaffnage
Dalry ✕Tyndrum
Perth
Dundee

Oban
(1306)
Balquhidder
St Andrews

Lorne
Strathearn
Cupar *Fife*

Argyll
Menteith
Stirling
Kinross

JURA
Lennox
Bannockburn
(1314)✕

Falkirk
Linlithgow
Edinburgh
Dunbar

ISLAY
Bothwell
Lothian

Kyle
Lanark

BUTE
Loudon Hill (1307)✕
Roxburgh
Berwick

Ayr
Galston ✕
Douglas

RATHLIN
ARRAN
Cumnock

Turnberry
Carrick
Northumberland

Dunaverty
Glen Trool
Dumfries
ENGLAND

Stranraer
Loch Ryan
Buittle
Caerlaverock

Galloway
Burgh-on-
Sands
Carlisle

Cumberland

24

5–Exile and Despair

When King Edward heard the news of Bruce's revolt he was outraged. He proclaimed that at the Feast of Pentecost, 22 May, he would knight his son, the Prince of Wales, who would in turn knight all eligible esquires – some 300 responded. They all swore, on two swans enmeshed in gold chains, never to rest until Scotland was subdued. The Prince of Wales set out to Carlisle at the head of a great army, while the ailing King followed. The English also petitioned the Pope for Robert Bruce to be excommunicated for his sacrilegious act in the church at Dumfries, and this sentence was passed by Pope Clement V on 18 May.

The Earl of Pembroke, Aymer de Valance, had already been instructed in April to march with Percy and Clifford against the rebels. His orders were to show no mercy to anyone associated with the revolt. Pembroke sped north with 3000 horsemen, joined by many of the dead Comyn's kin. He reached Perth unopposed early in June with 6000 men, capturing the Bishop of Glasgow at Cupar Castle in Fife; the Bishop of St Andrews surrendered at Kinross. They were imprisoned in England, their lives spared only because they were churchmen.

Bruce gathered support in the north, and approached Perth with 4500 men, arriving at the walls on 18 June. There he challenged Pembroke – in old chivalric tradition – to come outside and fight or surrender. Pembroke agreed to fight on the following morning. Bruce withdrew six miles to Methven, but as his men prepared to camp, the English attacked them and a desperate battle followed. Bruce escaped protected by a small group of knights, but his army suffered a heavy defeat. Many of his companions and followers were captured and brutally executed. The life of Thomas Randolph, a nephew of Bruce, was spared only on the condition that he fight for the English. In the wake of Pembroke's success, the Prince of Wales and his army of young knights ravaged the south of Scotland until all resistance there had been crushed.

With a handful of followers, Bruce fled into the mountains of Atholl, then turned west, reaching Tyndrum early in August. They were now in the domain of the MacDougall Lord of Lorne, a son-in-law of the dead Comyn, intent on avenging the death of his kinsman. The MacDougall clansmen hid at the mouth of the narrow pass at Dalry to which Bruce was headed. As Bruce's small force passed, Lorne's men attacked down each slope, slashing at the horses and riders with their axes. To escape, Bruce retreated along a narrow track, positioning himself at the rear of his men to defend them.

He sent his Queen, daughter and the other womenfolk to Kildrummy, escorted by Nigel Bruce and the Earl of Atholl. From there they were to join the Bishop of Moray in the Orkneys, while Nigel was to defend Kildrummy Castle for as long as possible.

Bruce and his men went south to avoid the lands of their enemies, leaving their armour behind and travelling on foot. They rested in caves at Balquhidder and Craigroyston, then crossed Loch Lomond, where they met the Earl of Lennox, who was loyal to Bruce. He took them to the coast, from where they sailed to Dunaverty on the tip of the Mull of Kintyre. There they were welcomed by Angus MacDonald of the Isles.

The Queen and her companions, meanwhile, had reached Kildrummy, only to be told that the Earl of Pembroke was at Aberdeen preparing to attack, so the royal ladies continued northward with the Earl of Atholl. When the Earl of Ross, a Comyn supporter, heard of their progress into Easter Ross, he attempted to capture them. They took refuge in the

St Duthac's Chapel, Tain

sanctuary of St Duthac at Tain, but were seized and sent to King Edward at Lanercost Priory.

Nigel Bruce was also captured by Pembroke and the Prince of Wales after the fall of Kildrummy Castle. The siege was ended by the treachery of the castle blacksmith – for the promise of English gold, he set the corn store on fire. The flames quickly spread to the castle gate, and the

English entered. After a day of fighting the defenders surrendered. The blacksmith was rewarded with as much gold as he could carry – the English poured it molten down his throat.

Nigel Bruce and the Earl of Atholl were hanged and beheaded. In response to pleas on behalf of the Earl of Atholl that he should receive special treatment on account of his royal blood, Edward had him hanged from a higher gallows than anybody else, and his head was placed on a pole higher than any other on London Bridge. The women were spared but imprisoned. Mary Bruce and Isabella, Countess of Buchan, were to spend the next four years in cages protruding from the battlements of Roxburgh and Berwick castles respectively. Marjorie and Christina Bruce were sent to convents, and the Queen was placed under house arrest for eight years at Burstwick-in-Holderness.

Bruce stayed only three days at Dunaverty – English forces under Sir John de Botetourt and Sir John Menteith were already on their way to besiege the castle. Bruce slipped away by boat and made for the island of Rathlin, off the north coast of Ireland. He was unheard of for almost five months, but probably spent his time recruiting support from the west Highlands and Islands. By the time he returned he had acquired a fleet of galleys and hundreds of men.

By January 1307 the English had discovered that Bruce was not at Dunaverty as they had thought. Edward ordered a fleet to hunt for him, but Bruce had already embarked on his return, aware of the capture of his family – but not their fate.

William Douglas had died in captivity eight years earlier in 1299. His son, James Douglas – just 12 years old – took a raiding party to Arran to steal provisions and arms from the governor, killing most of the garrison of Brodick Castle. Bruce joined them ten days later with 33 galleys. His brothers, Thomas and Alexander, were sent ahead to Galloway with 18 ships and several hundred men. Their plan was to break the English lines of communication between Carlisle and Ayr, but they were ambushed at Loch Ryan by the MacDowells of Galloway. All but two galleys were captured; Thomas and Alexander Bruce were taken to King Edward at Carlisle, where they were executed.

Bruce had also sent a man ahead to Carrick to assess the people's willingness to revolt – if he found them favourable he was to light a fire on Turnberry Point. On the agreed day a fire was seen from Arran and Bruce put his plan in motion. When he reached the shore, however, he was warned that somebody else had lit the fire, and that Turnberry Castle

Brodick Castle, Isle of Arran (see previous page), captured by James Douglas in 1307.

was garrisoned by Sir Henry Percy and several hundred English troops. Bruce decided not to turn back, but to attack the village at night while the soldiers slept. Only one Englishman escaped alive to the castle. Bruce captured much booty; Henry Percy remained within the castle, unsure of how many attackers were outside in the dark.

Bruce disappeared with his men into the mountains of Carrick, eluding capture and betrayal. He realised that he could never defeat his enemies – English or Scottish – with pitched battles and chivalric challenges. He would have to use guile, cunning and his knowledge of the terrain to fight a guerilla war. Followers slowly found their way to him, although much of Galloway and Ayrshire was occupied by English troops under the Earl of Pembroke.

During this time Bruce learned of his family's fate. Legend tells that as he lay dejected and grief-stricken in his cave, ready to give up the struggle and go to fight in the Holy Land instead, he saw a spider trying to make a web. The spider struggled to swing a thread to the wall, but persisted seven times until it succeeded. Bruce swore that if this tiny creature could try so hard, the King of Scots could do no less.

6–The Return of the King

By now Bruce's followers numbered 60, and they continued to elude the MacDowells of Galloway, John of Lorne and the Earl of Pembroke, while successfully carrying out night-time raids against their enemies.

James Douglas went to Douglasdale, where his hereditary castle was held by Sir Robert Clifford. On Palm Sunday, Douglas and a group of hand-picked local men disguised themselves and mingled with the garrison as they marched to the nearby church. Once there, to cries of *Douglas! Douglas!*, they attacked the English soldiers, and took them prisoner or slew them. Returning to the empty castle, Douglas and his followers ate the garrison's meal, then packed up as much booty as they could carry. They piled all the stores in the cellar, then beheaded the prisoners, and threw their heads on the pile. They fouled the well with dead horses and salt before setting the castle ablaze in what became known as *Douglas's Larder*, then returned to rejoin Bruce in the hills.

Pembroke withdrew to his base at Carlisle. Bruce moved into Galloway, making headquarters at Glen Trool. Early in April, the Earl of Pembroke learned of Bruce's position and sent 1500 knights to ambush the Scots. They approached Bruce's camp through woods, sending a woman into the camp to spy on their numbers, now totalling 300. But the woman lost her nerve and warned of the presence of the English. The Scots barely had time to arm themselves before the English rode out from the trees. Bruce shot an arrow through their leader's throat, and they pulled up abruptly; the Scots rushed forward and the English fled. The defeat was so shameful that the Earl of Pembroke retired to Carlisle in disgust.

The news of Bruce's triumph over 1500 English knights quickly spread, and supporters joined his band daily. Strong enough to leave the hills, he made his headquarters at Galston, near the English-held castle at Ayr, and controlled most of Kyle and Cunningham. An attempted attack by Sir Philip Mowbray with 1000 men was ambushed by Douglas, and this success brought even more volunteers to Bruce.

Urged on by King Edward from his sick bed, the Earl of Pembroke reassembled his troops and advanced on Galston. Bruce withdrew some miles to Loudon Hill. When the 3000-strong English army approached on the morning of 10 May, Bruce positioned his 600 spearmen across the road, behind ditches. The first English squadron to charge broke up trying to avoid the ditches. Those not killed or unhorsed turned back and collided with the second squadron. The Scots advanced steadily, routing Pembroke and his army, who fled to Bothwell Castle. Three days later Bruce attacked a relieving force under the Earl of Gloucester, inflicting heavy casualties.

King Edward, furious at the failure of his commanders to capture Bruce, was determined to do the job himself. He summoned troops to assemble at Carlisle on 8 July, and defied his illness to ride at their head. But the effort was too much, and having covered only six miles in four days, he reached the village of Burgh-on-Sands and died there on 11 July, having never again reached Scotland.

Edward's final wish was that his bones be carried at the head of his army into Scotland until the country had been subdued, but Edward II promptly abandoned his father's corpse at Waltham Abbey, to be buried later. He marched to Cumnock, stayed until 25 August, then returned to England, having never fought. It would be some years before he returned to Scotland, having more pressing problems at home. In the absence of their King, the English garrisons were content to stay within their castles.

Bruce was free to confront his Scottish enemies, primarily the MacDowells of Galloway; the MacDougalls of Lorne; the Earl of Ross; and the Earl of Buchan, leader of the Comyn supporters.

Dugald MacDowell had been responsible for the capture and death of Bruce's two brothers, Thomas and Alexander, and Bruce exacted a bloody revenge throughout Galloway. Many inhabitants fled to Cumbria, and those who remained were given the choice of paying tribute to Bruce or death.

In September the Earl of Pembroke was handing over the office of Viceroy to the Earl of Richmond, and Bruce seized the opportunity to break through the English-held line of the Clyde, leaving Douglas in command of the south-west. Gathering followers as he went, and supported from the sea by Angus MacDonald, Bruce confronted the MacDougalls in Argyll. Hoping to avoid a battle, he offered John of Lorne a temporary truce, which was accepted.

Bruce marched east through the Great Glen, capturing and destroying Inverlochy and Urquhart castles. He was supported by the Bishop of Moray, who had returned from the Orkneys and raised the men of Moray for Bruce. Together they seized and slighted Inverness Castle. In October Bruce persuaded the powerful Earl of Ross to accept a truce until June 1308. This left Bruce safe to attack the Comyns, who were headed by the Earl of Buchan.

Urquhart Castle, Loch Ness (see previous page)

Bruce marched as far as Inverurie, but fell seriously ill – his brother Edward ordered him carried in a litter to Slioch. The Earl of Buchan caught up with them on Christmas Day, and a running battle ensued until Buchan withdrew for reinforcements.

Edward Bruce took the chance to move the King to a safer position. He decided that the troops should boldly march out in full battle array with the King in a litter in their midst. They were so formidable a sight that Buchan let them leave untouched, and they reached the mountains of Strathbogie, where the local lord was friendly to Bruce's cause.

Over the winter, Bruce's strength returned and his army moved back down to Inverurie. Meanwhile Buchan had been reinforced by Sir David Brechin with men from Angus, and by Sir John Mowbray with an English force. In May 1308 Sir David Brechin attacked Bruce's outposts, sending them back to the main army at Inverurie. Bruce mounted his horse and led his men against Brechin's cavalry. At the sight of the King his enemies panicked and fled, closely pursued by Edward Bruce, who caught up with Mowbray and Buchan at Old Deer. After a fierce confrontation their men scattered in all directions, their leaders escaping to England. Sir David Brechin retreated to his castle at Brechin, where he was soon to change his allegiance. Edward Bruce ravaged the lands of Buchan – slaughtering men and livestock alike and burning crops and farms – so that the Comyns would never again pose a threat to Bruce.

By the summer of 1308, Douglas had gained control of much of the south-west, including his own lands, and he was able to push east into

Upper Clydesdale and the Selkirk Forest. At Peebles in July he captured Thomas Randolph, the King's nephew who had fought for the English since his capture at Methven. Douglas delivered Randolph to Bruce, and Randolph quickly changed his allegiance once again and begged Bruce's pardon. Randolph was to become one of Bruce's best commanders.

Bruce soon controlled most of eastern Scotland, and in July he gained a sea port when the people of Aberdeen revolted against the English. With the expiry of his truce with John of Lorne imminent, and English troops approaching from Carlisle, Edward Bruce was sent to Galloway to once more subdue the MacDowells. In late July Bruce marched to Argyll, and by mid-August he had reached the Pass of Brander, a narrow track

Kilchurn Castle, dating from the 15th century – the Pass of Brander is nearby

between Ben Cruachan and Loch Awe, through which he must pass to reach the lands of the MacDougalls.

John of Lorne had set an ambush by placing his men above the Pass. But Bruce was well prepared for this, and he sent Douglas with a force of Highlanders to a position higher above the men of Lorne. When the MacDougalls rose to attack Bruce's troops with boulders and arrows, they were brought down by a hail of arrows from above. At this moment, Bruce's men attacked from below. Taken by surprise and unable to defend their position on both sides, Lorne's men made for the single crossing of the River Awe. They tried to destroy the bridge behind them, but Bruce's men captured it intact and poured into the MacDougall's lands. John of Lorne escaped to England; his father surrendered Dunstaffnage Castle and was taken hostage.

Dunstaffnage Castle

Bruce returned to face the Earl of Ross. The Earl considered his position and on the last day of October surrendered and swore allegiance to Bruce.

Edward Bruce swept viciously through Galloway, and on 29 June at the River Dee routed a superior force led by Dugald MacDowell, Sir Ingram de Umfraville and Aymer St John. He was now joined by Douglas and Angus MacDonald.

Edward Bruce received word one morning that the English had made a forced march to surprise him. Edward took 50 knights to a position behind the English, under cover of a heavy mist. The mist suddenly cleared, revealing him to the enemy. Boldly he ordered an immediate charge, and although his knights were greatly outnumbered, they so surprised the enemy that they cut through them twice and had turned for a third onslaught when the English broke and fled.

The last of Bruce's Scottish enemies had been crushed, and he now controlled two-thirds of the country. Almost three years after his coronation, he could finally turn his attention to removing the English who remained in Scotland, and gaining international recognition of his sovereignty.

7–Uniting the Kingdom

Bruce came to St Andrews for his first parliament on 16 March 1309, the first free parliament convened in Scotland for 18 years. All the earldoms except Dunbar and Angus were represented, and also present were many members of the Church, and Bruce's commanders and knights.

One of the purposes of the parliament was to draft a reply to a letter from Philip IV of France. The French King had asked for the assistance of the Scots in a holy crusade, knowing that this would prevent Bruce from pursuing war with England. Philip had also written to Edward II, his son-in-law, suggesting a truce with the Scots to allow Edward to deal with his problems at home. A quarrel was raging between the English King and his leading nobles over Edward's boyhood friend, Piers Gaveston. The King's favourite regularly infuriated the barons, and at their insistence he was banished to Ireland in 1308.

Despite the reasoning behind Philip's letter, it was still important to Bruce in that his sovereignty had been recognised by the most important monarch in Europe. A reply was drafted to say that once Scotland was freed from the aggressions of the English, and had recovered from the ravages inflicted on them over many years, they would gladly join the King of France on his crusade. The clergy and nobles of Scotland then made declarations that King Robert was the true heir to Alexander III.

Edward II, however, was not prepared to acknowledge Bruce's sovereignty, and his attempts to negotiate a peace failed, as Bruce would accept no less. Edward set in motion plans for a full-scale invasion, prompted by repeated requests for assistance from his English-held castles in Scotland. In the autumn of 1309, two armies were sent north, but there was little appeal in a winter campaign and a truce was agreed until June 1310. Bruce took the opportunity to travel within the kingdom, making a royal progress down the west coast, and receiving homage from Highland chieftains.

Edward II's troubles were worsening. His nobles – calling themselves the Lords Ordainers – were attempting to impose reforms upon him. He had learned of the King of France's communications with Bruce, and wrote to his father-in-law accusing him of double-dealing. Philip responded by demanding that Edward go to France to do homage for his lands there, but Edward feared for the safety of Piers Gaveston, who had returned from Ireland. So in an attempt to avoid both the French King's summons and the Lords Ordainers, he and his favourite went north.

Edward issued a summons to all the English nobles and knights to assemble their armies at Berwick on 8 September 1310, and ships were ordered to bring provisions up the east coast. All the earls except Piers Gaveston, Earl of Cornwall, and the Earls of Gloucester and Surrey ignored the call to arms, but a sizeable army was still assembled.

For six weeks the English army marched throughout southern Scotland, but the enemy could not be found. The Scots had been well warned, and Bruce had withdrawn his army north of the Forth, leaving only raiding parties to harass the English. The country folk had taken to the hills with their stores and livestock, leaving a barren land.

Running low on provisions, Edward II turned back to Berwick in late October, and it was now that Bruce's raiding parties attacked the retreating army with full force, taking a heavy toll on their number. As soon as the English reached Berwick, Bruce invaded into English-held Lothian, but by the time the English army returned to confront them, the Scots had disappeared again.

Edward II and his army spent the next six months at Berwick, watching for renewed activity in Lothian and further avoiding the Lords Ordainers in the south. The result was a stalemate: Bruce slowly captured Ayr, while Edward refortified his English-held castles in Lothian and Galloway. In the summer of 1311, Edward was forced to withdraw to London to open parliament, at the insistence of the Lords Ordainers, leaving Piers Gaveston safe at Bamburgh Castle in Northumberland.

Bamburgh Castle

Bruce saw his opportunity to attack, and on 12 August he invaded into England across the Solway, burning much of the land and returning with a large number of cattle. He then travelled east and harried the lands of the Earl of Dunbar, before crossing into Northumberland for 15 days, burning and raiding as before.

Unable to defend themselves against the Scots, the Northumbrians offered to buy a truce. For £2000 this was granted until February 1312; Dunbar paid a similar price. As soon as the truces ended, the Scots attacked Norham Castle, across the Border from Berwick: both Northumberland and Dunbar immediately renewed their tributes.

By 1312, civil war had broken out in England. Piers Gaveston had been banished to Flanders in October 1311, but in January 1312 returned secretly to England. In an attempt to find a safe hiding place for him, Edward repeatedly sent envoys to Bruce. He offered better and better terms for a truce in return for Gaveston's residency in Scotland, but Bruce refused.

The Lords Ordainers marched north with their armies, and Piers Gaveston surrendered at Scarborough in May 1312 to the Earl of Pembroke, who had promised to spare his life. As he was being taken to Pembroke's castle, he was seized by the Earl of Warwick and beheaded by order of the Earl of Lancaster. The furious King and the Earl of Pembroke joined forces and marched against Lancaster.

Scarborough Castle

Taking advantage of the absence of English nobles from the northern counties, Bruce called a parliament at Ayr in July 1312. He decided on a much larger invasion of England. Again crossing the Solway, Bruce's troops raided from Lanercost Priory, near Carlisle, to Durham and Hartlepool, plundering and taking prisoners. The people of Durham offered £2000 for a truce until Midsummer 1313 – Bruce insisted that the Scots be granted free access through the county of Durham for raids further south. Northumberland quickly paid for the same truce, while Westmoreland, Coupland and Cumberland gave the sons of their chief lords as hostages for whatever they could not afford financially. As Midsummer 1313 drew near, Bruce sent representatives to each of the northern counties to threaten a renewal of the raids, and all of them bought further immunity until September 1314. Bruce received over £40 000 from such tributes over the three-year period.

In September 1312 the Scottish army returned from Durham. Leaving Edward Bruce in Galloway to harry the English garrisons there, and Douglas to police the Border and raid Lothian, Bruce went north to Inverness with Thomas Randolph. In October, at a parliament in Inverness, Bruce and envoys of the Norwegian King Haakon V renewed the ancient treaty between their two countries.

Since the St Andrews parliament of 1309, most of the English-held castles in Scotland had been captured, and Bruce decided to take the remainder. Leaving a force to besiege Perth, he rode south and attempted a surprise capture of Berwick. On 6 December 1312 he and his men used special rope ladders fitted with grappling hooks to scale the walls, but a barking dog alerted the people of Berwick to their presence. After this failure, Bruce swiftly returned to the siege of Perth.

By January 1313, Perth had not weakened. The Scots secretly found a place where they could wade across the moat. Bruce then lifted the siege, withdrawing to a nearby wood. On the night of 7 January the Scots returned, wading through the moat, which came up to their shoulders. Bruce himself led the silent assault on the walls, and by dawn the surprised defenders had surrendered. Bruce ordered that the castle and town be burned to the ground.

A month later Dumfries Castle surrendered, and by 31 March Caerlaverock and Buittle had also fallen. Outside Lothian and the Borders, only Bothwell and Stirling remained under English control. Bothwell could wait, but the strategically essential Stirling had to be taken, and Edward Bruce was put in charge of laying siege to it, while King Robert busied himself with capturing the Isle of Man.

In the summer of 1313, bored and frustrated by the long profitless siege of Stirling Castle, Edward Bruce struck a deal with Sir Philip Mowbray, the warden of the castle for the English. If the garrison was not relieved by noon on Midsummer's Day, 1314, they would surrender to the Scots – a bold and chivalrous agreement which appealed to the romantic in the King's brother.

Although such agreements were not uncommon, Edward's deal with Mowbray was definitely not part of Bruce's pragmatic strategy of guerrilla warfare and covert assault. As King, he had to honour the bargain, but his unease was clear – he knew that Edward II could never ignore such a challenge. Barbour, in the epic 14th-century poem *The Brus*, gives the King these words: *That was unwisely done indeed ... We are so few against so many. God may deal us our destiny right well but we are set in jeopardy to lose or win all at one throw.*

Edward Bruce's treaty was a godsend to the English King. It provided a rallying cry to his rebellious nobles and promised an easy victory. Starting in the autumn of 1313, Edward II laid his plans and issued a call to arms. Ireland and Wales were pacified, and English relations with France for the time being were cordial. In October, Edward pardoned the Earl of Lancaster, and turned his full military might against Scotland.

Bruce, too, was not idle. He moved swiftly, taking and destroying Scottish castles which still remained in English hands. Despite the heavy English presence in Lothian and the Borders, most of the Scottish inhabitants believed in Bruce. It was often with their help that Bruce's lieutenants were able to capture English strongholds.

On 27 February 1314, the garrison of Roxburgh Castle were celebrating Shrove Tuesday with a feast. In the dark, Douglas and 60 men disguised themselves as stray cattle, wearing black cloaks and crawling on hands and knees. Ignored by the sentries, they were able to approach the castle walls and hook up scaling ladders. Silently they climbed over the walls, killing a sentry before he could raise the alarm. To cries of *Douglas! Douglas!* they swarmed into the great hall where the feast was being held, and the startled garrison took fright and fled.

Douglas and Randolph shared a friendly rivalry, and not to be outdone by his friend, Randolph was intent on capturing Edinburgh Castle, which is perched on a steep rock. Weeks of siege had yielded nothing, and Randolph offered a reward to anyone who knew a way up the rock-face. He found William Francis, who as a youth had lived in the castle. He had often climbed up and down the rock when secretly visiting his sweetheart in the town, and offered to lead Randolph and his men. Randolph instructed the rest of his force to assault the south gate when he gave the signal from within the castle.

On the night of 14 March, they climbed the north face, clinging to the rock. Pausing to rest on a ledge, the Scots were horrified to hear a voice cry out, *Away, I see you!*, as a stone thrown from above bounced past

Capture of Edinburgh Castle (Catriona Campbell)

Edinburgh Castle

them down the crag. Fortunately for the Scots, the voice belonged to a practical joker amongst the English, who wished to startle his companions. As he and the other sentries moved on, the Scots began to climb again.

At last, they reached the top, and set up the rope ladder they had brought to scale the 12-foot-high wall. William Francis was first, followed by Sir Andrew Gray and Randolph. The English, alerted by the clatter of arms and armour, raised the alarm and rushed to repel the Scots. Randolph's main force, hearing the cries from within, ran out of hiding to assault the south gate. Fighting hand to hand every step of the way, Randolph and his men slowly cut their way towards them. A short, vicious battle ensued around the gate. The English captain of the castle was slain, and the gate opened. In poured the Scots, and the English garrison was overwhelmed. History does not tell us the fate of the garrison's resident practical joker. In line with Bruce's strategy, the castle was demolished to prevent it from falling back into enemy hands.

The capture of Edinburgh castle marked the final end of English power in Lothian. When Edward II came north to relieve Stirling, only a handful of Scottish castles remained in English hands.

8–Bannockburn

Just before Christmas 1313, Edward began to issue his summons, commanding eight earls and 87 barons to assemble, with their retinues, at Berwick on 10 June. In March 1314 he increased his activity, issuing orders levying some 15 000 infantry from the north and Midlands, 3000 archers from Wales, and organising the provision of over 200 carts and wagons. Over 2500 mounted knights, heavily armed and armoured, came at Edward's call, each bringing two or three mounted men-at-arms to share in the inevitable English victory. Fully assembled, the English army numbered over 20 000 men, superbly equipped and ready for battle.

Confidence was high: at Berwick, Edward parcelled out Scottish lands to various favourites, sure that they would soon be in his power. The English King promised houses and castles in Scotland to many of his knights and nobles, who brought furniture and tapestries with them for their new homes.

Bruce, too, made his preparations. By the beginning of May 1314, he had established his headquarters near Stirling, ending all other Scottish military campaigns. He summoned fighting men from across the kingdom, and little by little the Scottish army grew.

As they waited, Bruce trained his men and appointed captains. The vanguard – the position of honour – was commanded by Randolph, and probably numbered around 500 men. The second division was led by Edward Bruce and numbered around 1000. The third division, roughly the same size as the second, was under the nominal command of the young Walter Stewart, the hereditary High Steward of Scotland. As he was not yet of age, the captain in all but name was his cousin, Douglas, who was himself only 19. Then came the King's own division: 2000 Highlanders, clansmen from the north and west under Angus MacDonald, as well as men from Bruce's own lands in Kyle and Carrick. Lastly came the Scottish cavalry: 500 light horse commanded by the Marischal, Sir Robert Keith; and a small company of archers from the Ettrick forest.

The Scottish soldiers were – apart from Keith's cavalry – entirely on foot. They were each armed with a 12-foot-long spear, the same type that had conquered at Stirling Bridge but failed at Falkirk, and probably a sword or dirk. They wore heavily padded leather armour, or perhaps chain mail. Most would have had a steel helmet. The Scottish knights, lightly armed and armoured, could not match the weight or force of their

English counterparts, but were certainly faster and more manoeuvrable. The archers from the Ettrick forest were skilled, but their light bows were toys compared to the Welsh longbows – which could, from long range, drive an arrow through the oaken door of a castle or through the body of a fully armoured knight. All in all, the Scots numbered about 5000 or 6000 men – roughly a quarter the size of the English army – and were less well equipped.

The Scottish army was, however, very well prepared. Many of Bruce's men had fought with him for years, and his captains had often shown their abilities. As soon as new recruits arrived, they were trained and disciplined and made into strong, reliable fighting units.

Bruce had selected the best possible site on which to fight, choosing a position just north of the Torwood, in the valley of the Bannock burn, across the road to Stirling. To the east was the broad, flat Carse of Balquiderock, a triangle of firm land between the Pelstream and the Bannock burns, where they met and flowed together. Eastwards from the Carse was a marshland, covered in meandering streams, and beyond that the broad River Forth. The English could not easily cross such terrain without exposing themselves to the kind of slaughter they had suffered at Stirling Bridge. To the west lay the Torwood and beyond that the forest of the New Park, also impenetrable to the English. They would have to come from the south. If they crossed the Bannock Burn at the ford directly south of Bruce's position, they would immediately face the Scottish defences. To prevent the English from spreading out when they emerged from the forest, the Scots dug numerous pits on either side of the road, each just deep enough to make the area impassable to horsemen. If they came this way, the English would have to fight on a very narrow front indeed. The other possible route was along the trackway that crossed the Carse, but here they would find themselves with the Scots on a hill overlooking their left flank. The English would not pass easily.

Edward II's progress was a lot less smooth. By 21 June – Midsummer, the day by which he had to relieve Stirling Castle, was on 24 June – he had only reached Edinburgh. The next day, his army made a forced march 22 miles to Falkirk in the full heat of summer, arriving parched, dusty and exhausted, ten miles and a day and a half away from the battle.

By 22 June the Scots knew the English had come: thousands upon thousands of knights and footsoldiers with columns of wagons stretching into the distance, raising a great plume of dust across the horizon. Bruce kept this news to himself and his commanders, and told his men only that the enemy was approaching in great disorder.

The *small folk*, camp followers consisting largely of wives, mothers and children, cooks and prostitutes, grooms, squires, labourers and servants, were sent with the supply train behind Coxet Hill for safety. With them went men who had arrived too late to be integrated into the trained fighting units, who were to protect the small folk and to act as a reserve. Randolph's men were stationed by St Ninian's Kirk to watch the track which ran across the Carse. Edward Bruce and Douglas stood along the eastern edge of the hill overlooking the Carse, while the King remained at the south guarding the road from the ford. Keith's cavalry remained in the centre, where they could rapidly reach any part of the army if needed. Although purely defensive, the Scottish position was undoubtedly superior: the English would have to fight on Bruce's terms.

Next morning, just after the early

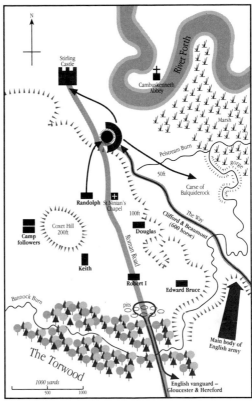

23 June 1314: The English vanguard is checked and repulsed; Bruce slays de Bohun; Randolph engages and defeats English knights under Clifford & Beaumont. The main body of the English army takes up position at the head of the Carse.

summer dawn, Bruce proclaimed that if any man was afraid, let him leave at once. The Scottish army roared out their reply: they would conquer or die. Around noon, the English army reached the Torwood. Their plan was to send the vanguard, under the joint command of the Earls of Gloucester and Hereford, along the Roman road leading to Stirling Castle. The Scots, they believed, would probably retire when faced by so large an army, so a second group of around 500 to 600 knights, led by Sir Robert Clifford and Sir Henry Beaumont, was sent along the track across the Carse to cut off their retreat. Secure in the knowledge that they were vastly superior to the Scots in both numbers and material, the English advanced boldly.

The English vanguard moved forward swiftly. The leading knights, eager for battle, sighted the Scots across the valley, and assumed that they were withdrawing. They forded the Bannock burn, their horses surging through the water, their weapons and armour gleaming in the afternoon sunshine. Sir Henry de Bohun, nephew of the Earl of Hereford, spied a glint of gold about the head of one of the Scots who, mounted on a small, sturdy grey, was obviously in command. This could only be the King of Scots himself: de Bohun couched his lance and spurred his warhorse into a charge.

Robert Bruce caught sight of de Bohun's approach. He had two options: retreat to safety behind the Scottish defences, or meet the attack head-on. Armed only with a battle-axe, he wheeled his horse around and rode towards the English knight. At the last second, he swerved to his left, avoiding the lance; standing up in his stirrups, he smashed his axe across de Bohun's face, cutting through his helmet and splitting his head in two. The axe handle shattered with the force of the blow. Henry de Bohun fell to the ground, dead.

Bruce's men, seeing their King perform this amazing feat of arms, let out a tremendous yell and surged forward to meet the rest of the English vanguard as they emerged from the wood. The English were in disarray, many of them falling into the hidden pits. The sudden wild charge caught them unawares, and a fierce fight ensued. The Earl of Gloucester himself was thrown and only saved from death or capture by his squires. The English knights retreated in confusion. The Scots began exultantly to pursue them, but Bruce called them back – a striking example of how well he had trained his men.

The Scottish commanders crowded around the King, anxious for his health after his duel with de Bohun, and rebuking him for having placed

Bruce and de Bohun (Catriona Campbell)

himself in such mortal danger. Bruce did not answer them; his only comment was that he regretted breaking his axe. Then, on the Carse below, Clifford, Beaumont and their knights were spotted moving along the track towards St Ninian's Kirk, threatening to outflank the Scottish army. Randolph hurried back to his men; marshalling them together, he led them out onto the open ground to contest the English advance.

The English knights manoeuvred to surround the Scots. Randolph

45

formed his men into a hollow circle, presenting a hedge of long spears all around. Several knights impaled themselves and their horses trying to break up the Scottish formation, without success. The English rode round and around, hurling swords, maces and axes in anger and frustration. Again and again the Scottish soldiers would lunge forwards, spearing a knight, or more usually his horse, and bringing him to the ground. The air filled with dust and with the cries and screams of wounded and dying men. Douglas, seeing his friend surrounded, asked for permission to go to his aid, but Bruce, wary of a second English attack, refused. Still the battle continued. Again, Douglas made his request; this time, the King gave him leave to go to his friend's rescue.

Douglas and his men moved towards the battle. As they approached, the English began to waver. Randolph seized his chance and drove his men forward, crashing through the encircling knights and splitting them apart. Some fled north to seek refuge in Stirling Castle, while the rest ran south towards the main body of their army. Seeing this, Douglas halted his men, saying, *The Earl of Moray has gained the day and, since we were not there to help him, let us leave to him the honour of the victory.* Randolph and his men marched back to the Scottish army, weary but triumphant.

After Clifford had returned to the English army with news of his defeat, it was clear that no further action could be taken that day. The English commanders decided to bivouac between the Bannock and Pelstream burns, where they would be protected from any night attack. In the morning, the Scots would face the full might of the English cavalry across the hard, level ground of the Carse; the English would then charge the Scottish defences and obliterate them. But to reach their campsite they had to negotiate a marshland criss-crossed by innumerable streams and rivulets. By the time they had all arrived at their positions, the short summer night was all but over. Denied the chance to sleep, the knights stood by their horses, fully armed and armoured.

That night, Bruce and his commanders debated their options. The first day had brought them notable success, yet still they faced an enemy many times their size and power. For years, Bruce had deliberately avoided pitched battle. All his previous experience must have been telling him to slip away in the night, leaving the English army to return home in frustration with what little booty they could extract from the impoverished countryside. And yet here was a glorious opportunity to confirm his Kingship through triumph on the field of battle. The English forces were exhausted and demoralised after two forced marches and two defeats; if he was ever to defeat the English, now was the time.

The English expected Bruce to remain behind his defences to receive the English cavalry charge – no one could sensibly expect foot soldiers to take the offensive against such a force. Yet the encounter between Randolph and Clifford had shown that a well ordered and determined formation of spearmen could face and overcome even the most experienced knights. The English positions placed them in a tight pocket of land between the Pelstream and the Bannock burns, giving them no room to manoeuvre and cancelling out the threat of their cavalry. Bruce's tactical genius was to overturn the assumptions of the past and create a new kind of warfare. The Scottish army would attack.

24 June 1314 – Midsummer's Day and the Feast of St John the Baptist. On this the longest day of the year, dawn broke shortly before 4 am. The Scottish priests celebrated Mass, and the troops ate a light meal as befitted a holy day. As they assembled into their divisions – flying many banners to disguise their small numbers – the King, according to custom, called forth and knighted those whom he had chosen for the honour, among them James Douglas. The Abbot of Inchaffray, holding the Monymusk Reliquary, a silver casket containing the bones of St Columba, then blessed the Scottish knights and soldiers. A moment of silence; then Bruce gave the order to advance.

The Scottish forces were drawn up in schiltron formation, presenting a dense thicket of spears towards the enemy. Edward Bruce commanded the leading division, and marched towards the English positions, his right flank protected by the Bannock burn. Then, to his left and a little further back, Thomas Randolph; finally, to his left and

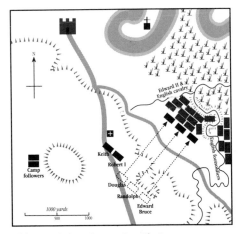

24 June 1314, early morning: The Scots advance, confining the English cavalry.

further back again, James Douglas. The King and his division remained with the Scottish cavalry, in reserve on the slopes of the hill.

Edward II and most of his army were amazed at this tactic. *What, will yonder Scots fight?* exclaimed the English King. As he spoke, the Scottish troops knelt briefly in prayer. Edward crowed, *They kneel for mercy!* Sir Ingram de Umfraville, a former Guardian of Scotland now fighting with the English because of his loyalties to Balliol and the Comyns, replied, *For mercy, yes, but not from you: from God and for their sins. These men will win all or die.*

So be it, replied Edward, and ordered his army to assemble. The Earl of Gloucester, his pride dented by the events of the previous day, was so eager to answer the call to battle that he charged Edward Bruce's division before the rest of his men had assembled. He died, impaled on the Scottish spears. Many of the English vanguard, scrambling piecemeal in his wake, suffered the same fate.

The Scottish spearmen were too strong to be broken. As the schiltrons commanded by Randolph and Douglas arrived on the English flank, the whole vanguard broke and fled in confusion back to the main body of their cavalry, their panicked and often riderless horses preventing their companions from forming a cohesive force. The pride of

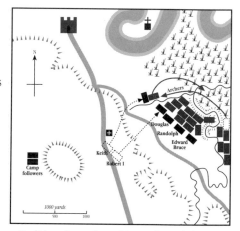

English archers take position and attack the Scottish left flank, but are dispersed by Keith's cavalry. Bruce commits his reserve to the battle.

English chivalry was reduced to a confused mass of men and horses, trapped by the two waterways and facing a steadily advancing wall of Scottish spears. Unable to cross the streams and blocked by their own cavalry, the English footsoldiers could lend no assistance.

At Falkirk in 1298 Edward I had used Welsh longbowmen to deadly effect against the Scottish schiltrons. But here they could not fire without hitting their own cavalry. Eventually they were brought into position, and they began to pour arrows into Douglas and Randolph's left flank. This manoeuvre might have saved the day for Edward II, but Bruce saw the danger and sent Sir Robert Keith with his small body of light cavalry to attack and disperse them. The archers, with no protection from this attack, were cut down and driven away. The survivors fled back to the main body of the English infantry, many of whom began to panic.

The English knights, their backs to the water, fought desperately. The Scots had the advantage of territory, but the English army was still enormously powerful. Bruce decided to send in his reserve, committing all his forces either to victory or to defeat. He turned to Angus MacDonald, saying, *My hope is constant in thee.* MacDonald and his clansmen flung themselves into battle, crashing into the beleaguered enemy. Their added weight and the force of their charge drove the English back still further, and a great cry of *On them! On them! They fail, they fail!* rose up from the Scottish army.

Defeat now was certain for the English. Edward II – still fighting bravely – was dragged away from the battle. The English defeat, disastrous though it was, would have been catastrophic if Edward had fallen into Scottish hands. With a bodyguard of 500 knights, he fought his way across the ebbing Pelstream burn and escaped towards Stirling Castle.

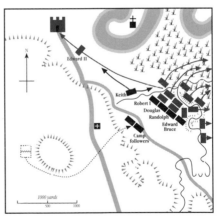

The sight of Edward and the Royal Standard in retreat was too much for the English. To add to their distress, the Scottish

Edward II is forced to flee. This, and the arrival of the camp followers, panics the English army into headlong flight.

camp followers, bearing improvised banners and weaponry, emerged from behind Coxet Hill, cheering and shouting. Faced with what must have seemed a second Scottish army, the English became a panic-stricken mob and their slow retreat became a headlong rout. Every mounted knight and noble left alive spurred their horses and fled. Many were captured by the Scots. Others, less fortunate, were crushed in the rout or drowned in the Bannock burn, which became choked with the bodies of the dead and the dying. Only the Earl of Pembroke salvaged his honour by returning to the battlefield to marshal the Welsh archers, men from his own Earldom, and lead them safely home. The rest of the English infantry scattered in all directions.

Edward II reached Stirling Castle safely, only to find that the governor, Sir Philip Mowbray, would not let him in. As he explained, he would have to surrender the castle, and the King would become a Scottish prisoner. He did, however, send out a knight who knew the area to lead Edward safely back to England.

Hearing of Edward II's escape, Bruce sent Douglas with 60 knights in pursuit. Douglas caught up with the English King and his retinue at Linlithgow; the 500 English knights were too strong to be taken in battle, so Douglas contented himself with a remorseless and ruthless pursuit. Any English knight who strayed or straggled behind was swiftly captured or killed. The Scots followed them so closely that, according to Barbour, *the English knights had not even leisure to make water*, and, reaching Dunbar, they abandoned their horses outside the castle gates rather than risk capture themselves.

Edward Bruce was sent in pursuit of the English nobles who had fled to Bothwell Castle, to cut them off or to besiege the castle if they reached it first. There were many noble prisoners to deal with, who could be ransomed back to their families for sizeable sums of money. Bruce's old friend, Raoul de Monthermer, and Sir Marmaduke Tweng, veteran of the Scottish wars

Bothwell Castle

and one of the few English survivors of the battle of Stirling Bridge, were released without ransom. Sir Philip Mowbray, after surrendering Stirling Castle, pledged his allegiance to the Scottish King.

More captives were to come. Walter FitzGilbert, Governor of Bothwell Castle, was a Scot who had sided with the English. He admitted a large body of fleeing English cavalry, then promptly changed sides and made them all prisoners. These captives included many great and powerful lords, including Humphrey de Bohun, Earl of Hereford and Constable of England. For the return of Hereford alone, Bruce was able to ransom his Queen, Elizabeth de Burgh; his daughter Marjorie; his sister Christina; and Robert Wishart, Bishop of Glasgow – as well as 11 other friends and family members held captive in England.

The Scots also took the enormous baggage train brought by the English, which was said to have stretched 20 miles. As well as arms and armour, tents and clothing, war horses and pack animals, the booty included wine, corn and hay, flocks of sheep and herds of pigs. There were also chests of money, gold and silver plate, and the English King's personal goods and treasure. Edward II also lost his shield and his privy seal, which – with ironic courtesy – Bruce returned to him. In total the booty alone was worth over £200 000 – over £50 million in today's currency. Scotland, impoverished by 18 years of warfare, became rich overnight. Bruce's generosity in distributing the spoils amongst all his men spread the benefits of victory across his kingdom.

Bannockburn was a hugely important victory to the Scots, and a catastrophic defeat for the English. It broke forever the power of the Scottish nobles who opposed Bruce and united the kingdom behind him. But it did not bring peace: Edward II still refused to acknowledge Bruce as King of Scots or Scotland as a separate, independent kingdom. A great battle had been won, but the war continued.

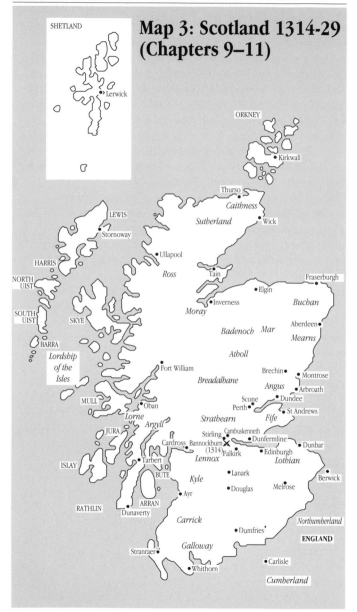

Map 3: Scotland 1314-29 (Chapters 9–11)

SHETLAND

Lerwick

ORKNEY

Kirkwall

Thurso

Caithness

Sutherland

Wick

LEWIS

Stornoway

Ullapool

HARRIS

NORTH UIST

Ross

Tain

Elgin

Fraserburgh

SOUTH UIST

SKYE

Inverness

Moray

Buchan

BARRA

Lordship of the Isles

Badenoch

Mar

Aberdeen

Mearns

Atholl

Fort William

Breadalbane

Brechin

Montrose

Angus

Arbroath

MULL

Oban

Scone

Perth

Dundee

St Andrews

Lorne

Argyll

Strathearn

Fife

JURA

Stirling

Cambuskenneth

Cardross

Bannockburn (1314)

Dunfermline

ISLAY

Tarbert

Falkirk

Edinburgh

Dunbar

Lennox

Lothian

BUTE

Kyle

Lanark

Berwick

ARRAN

Ayr

Douglas

Melrose

RATHLIN

Dunaverty

Carrick

Northumberland

ENGLAND

Galloway

Dumfries

Stranraer

Whithorn

Carlisle

Cumberland

9–Into Ireland and England

In the wake of their victory, the Scots were impatient for action. In August 1314 Bruce's troops – led by Edward Bruce, James Douglas and John Soulis – raided through Northumberland, County Durham, Yorkshire and Cumberland, gathering booty and receiving tribute. Such raids became regular and frequent throughout the coming years, and the inhabitants of the northern counties of England, who received no aid from their King, suffered greatly.

At a parliament at Cambuskenneth in November, it was decreed that any landowner who did not do homage to King Robert would forfeit his lands – most of Bruce's former enemies chose to become loyal subjects of the Scottish King.

In December, Bruce himself led another invasion into England, this time along the Tyne valley, and the people of the area paid for a truce until Midsummer 1315. A third raid deep into County Durham, led by Douglas and Randolph, followed in early 1315. By now the English were so demoralised that they offered no resistance.

In an attempt to attack the English on another front, Bruce sent envoys to Ireland offering to assist them in regaining their liberty from the English. For many years the English had controlled Ireland, using it as a supply of men and resources for the war against the Scots. The royal line of Ulster – the O'Neills – responded, and in return they offered the throne of Ireland to Edward Bruce.

This offer would have appealed to Bruce in two ways. Establishing a force in Ireland would give him a strategic point from which to attack southern England or join forces with the Welsh. It would also put some distance between himself and his brother, who was often impetuous and harboured jealous ambitions to the Scottish throne. At Ayr in April 1315, a parliament decided to send Edward Bruce to Ireland, accompanied by Thomas Randolph, with a force of 6000 men.

The parliament also decided upon the succession to the Scottish throne. Robert Bruce had no legitimate son, and the country needed a strong leader to keep the English at bay. Edward Bruce would succeed King Robert in the event of his death without a male heir. Following him in succession would be Edward's male heirs, and if none, the throne would fall to Marjorie Bruce and her heirs. With the issue safely decided, Edward Bruce sailed for Ireland, landing at Larne on 26 May 1315.

King Robert himself sailed to the Western Isles where John of Lorne had been trying to gather support for the English King. Bruce and Walter Stewart sailed up Loch Fyne and, to avoid sailing all the way around the Mull of Kintyre, laid pine trees across the narrow strip of land between East and West Tarbert. Dragging their ships, they crossed to the open sea. An ancient prophecy that whoever sailed across the land would rule the men of the Isles appeared to have been fulfilled, and men flocked to do homage to Bruce. John of Lorne retired to England without supporters.

The men of the Islands now harried the English coastal towns, and when a rumour spread that Edward Bruce was preparing to cross to Wales to help them against the English, the Welsh rebelled. With his attention required in the west, Edward II was unable to reinforce the north, and it was now that Bruce chose to strike.

On 22 July he laid siege to Carlisle Castle, and for the first time brought a siege engine with him. But the garrison of the castle had eight such devices, and easily repelled the Scottish assault. On 30 July, Bruce tried a

Map 4: England & Ireland

surprise attack on the eastern wall, but was thwarted by the defending archers. Abandoning his siege equipment in the mud, he hastily returned to Scotland.

Bruce and James Douglas attempted another surprise attack at night, in January 1316, this time on Berwick, but they were spotted in the moonlight and repelled. In February, a group of knights from the town were foraging for food in Teviotdale when James Douglas – who was building a hunting lodge in the Selkirk Forest – learned of their presence and rode to confront them. Despite finding himself greatly outnumbered, Douglas fought ferociously until his opponents were slain or had fled.

Tragedy struck the Bruce family on 2 March 1316. The King's heavily pregnant daughter Marjorie was thrown from her horse and killed. Surgeons cut her open and delivered the infant Robert Stewart from her body: many years later he would be crowned Robert II, first of the Stewart Kings.

In the summer, following a period of mourning, Bruce led a profitable raid through Yorkshire. Three months later he turned his attentions to Ireland once again. Randolph had brought news that Edward Bruce awaited his brother's arrival with reinforcements.

Since his arrival in Ireland, Edward Bruce had successfully defeated the Anglo-Irish leaders in the north in successive battles, despite the repeated treachery of the Irish chieftains, often more concerned with their own in-fighting than with defeating the English. He had failed, however, to penetrate the English-held south and west, and it was with this aim that Robert Bruce crossed to Carrickfergus in the autumn with a sizeable army.

Edward Bruce had been crowned High King of Ireland on 2 May 1316 at Dundalk, and it was customary for the new king to make a royal progress through the provinces. Thus two divisions left Carrickfergus in February 1317, with Edward Bruce commanding the front, and Robert Bruce at the rear. They moved south, but it was not long before they encountered an ambush laid by the Anglo-Irish barons, led by the Red Earl of Ulster, Robert Bruce's father-in-law.

The two divisions had already separated. Edward Bruce – impetuous as always – had eagerly pushed ahead. The enemy waiting in the woods allowed him to pass, but Robert Bruce spotted two archers stepping out of the trees and quickly ordered his troops to line up in battle formation. The enemy emerged from the woods in their hundreds, and although the Scots were outnumbered eight to one, they fought hard until the

Anglo-Irish retreated to Dublin. Bruce decided against a siege of the city, returning instead to his camp at Castleknock.

At the suggestion of Brian Ban O'Brien, an Irish chieftain from the south-west, Bruce rode towards Limerick. O'Brien had promised that the people of Munster would revolt upon Bruce's arrival, but instead he found himself opposed by Murrough O'Brien, Brian O'Brien's clan rival. Thwarted once again by clan feuds, fearful of the famine which gripped the land, and hearing that the new Lord Lieutenant of Ireland, Sir Roger Mortimer, was gathering troops to block his return to Ulster, Bruce ordered a retreat.

The journey north was thoroughly miserable, through lands desolated by famine and plague, but eventually they arrived in Ulster. Bruce had to return to Scotland, and leaving many of his men with his brother, he and Randolph sailed for Scotland, landing late in May 1317.

In October 1318 Edward Bruce planned an attack on Dundalk. By now he had enlisted the support of several Irish chieftains, and was expecting reinforcements from Scotland. But true to his nature, Edward Bruce was too impatient to await the arrival of more troops. He mounted his attack with a diminished force, for the native Irish refused to fight. At the first onslaught the meagre group of Scots was annihilated: Edward Bruce and most of his men were killed. With his death, attempts to establish a regime in Ireland ended, but the English never again used it as a base from which to attack Scotland.

Following several failed English incursions into Scotland, Edward II sought help from the new Pope, John XXII. In the absence of any Scots – who were barred by their excommunication – the English envoys convinced the Pope that only the stubbornness of the Scots and their refusal to make peace prevented the English from joining a crusade. The Pope immediately demanded a two-year truce, and letters were sent to the English and Scottish Kings late in the autumn of 1317.

The letters were delivered by two envoys whom Robert Bruce received with courtesy. When he saw that the letters were addressed not to the King of Scots, but to *Robert Bruce, acting as King of Scots*, he returned them unopened. The envoys were forced to return with the letters. Another emissary was dispatched, but when Bruce saw that the address was unchanged, he refused the letters again. The envoy was attacked on the road to Berwick, and his clothes and documents stolen. It was rumoured that the papers were now in the possession of the Scottish King.

Bruce turned his attentions to capturing Berwick. One of the burgesses sent word to Sir Robert Keith that when it was his turn to keep watch on the wall, he would let the Scots in. Bruce told Keith to assemble his men at Duns Park, keeping the plan secret. He sent Douglas and Randolph with a few men to join him. On the night of 1 April 1318, they crept to the wall and scaled it with ladders. There they were supposed to await the arrival of Bruce with reinforcements, but by the morning Douglas and Randolph could not prevent their men from plundering the town. In the panic many of the townsfolk fled to the castle, rousing the garrison. Douglas and Randolph fought almost single-handedly until the English were forced back to the castle.

Reinforcements soon arrived under Bruce and secured the town. Within three months the castle was starved into surrender. Bruce did not destroy the stronghold as usual, but instead repaired and improved it, knowing how important it was to control Berwick. He placed Walter Stewart in command, who installed catapults and hoses for discharging Greek fire – a kind of medieval napalm.

Since the death of Edward Bruce in Ireland there was now no confirmed heir to the Scottish throne. A parliament at Scone in December 1318 chose the infant Robert Stewart, Bruce's grandson, to be his successor, with Randolph as Regent.

In June 1319, Edward II and the Earl of Lancaster gathered forces at

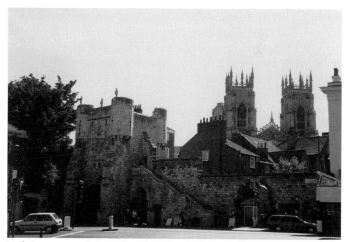

York (see next page). It was from here that the Scots tried to seize Queen Isabella.

Newcastle and prepared to march on Berwick, leaving Queen Isabella at York. The English army numbered 12 000, and when they arrived at Berwick they formed a huge encampment around the walls. On 7 September the assault began, but the English were unable to break through. At night they withdrew to their camp. Five days later they attacked again, from land and sea, but despite heavy losses the Scots again defended throughout the day.

Bruce was unable to breach the English forces to relieve the city, but was aware that England itself had been left wide open. He planned to capture Queen Isabella at York and use her as a hostage to negotiate a peace. Douglas and Randolph sped south to join up with Scottish spies in York, but one of these spies was captured and under torture revealed the plot. The Archbishop of York made sure that the Queen was safely sent to Nottingham then – with a following of citizens and clergymen – chose to attack the Scots, who were hiding in a wood near Mitton.

This makeshift English army approached in great disarray. The Scots saw them coming and set fire to much hay, hiding them from their enemy. The Scots formed into a single schiltron, and advanced as the smoke cleared. The Archbishop's men fled, but 300 were still killed. This skirmish became known as the *Chapter of Mitton*, because of the number of clergymen slain. The Scots spread throughout Yorkshire, burning and pillaging. Edward II considered turning south to protect the northern counties, but under pressure from the southern nobles chose to pursue the siege. The Earl of Lancaster left in disgust, taking his troops with him. As these made up one third of the army, Edward II was forced to raise the siege, and return to England. No sooner had the English army disbanded in November, than Douglas was leading his most savage raid yet on Westmoreland and Cumberland, burning the harvest and taking hostages and livestock.

Faced with the repeated failure of his armies and the constant suffering of his northern people, Edward II now succumbed to opening negotiations for a truce. Envoys met at Berwick on 22 December 1319, agreeing terms for a two-year truce from 1 January 1320.

10–Treaties and Conspiracies

The English King now renewed his pressure on the Pope, who summoned Bruce and his churchmen to Avignon, but once again the letter was not addressed to the King of Scots, and so was refused. In retaliation, the Pope ordered the English bishops to repeat the notices of excommunication against Bruce and also against the Scottish bishops.

Prompted by the Pope's actions, the people of Scotland sent him a letter, on 6 April 1320, known as the Declaration of Arbroath. It is believed to have been written by Bernard Linton, Chancellor of Scotland and Abbot of Arbroath, and carried the seals of eight earls and 31 barons.

Declaration of Arbroath

The Declaration briefly outlined the history of the Scots and of their struggle with the kings of England. It then described how Robert Bruce had emerged as a leader to free the Scots from English oppression, and how the people acknowledged him as their true and rightful monarch. The letter ended with a promise that, should the English cease all aggression towards them, the Scots would gladly join with a crusade to the Holy Land.

The Pope succumbed to this emotive plea from the Scots, writing to Edward II that he should immediately make peace with the Scots. Papal, Scottish, English and French envoys were appointed to negotiate a lasting peace, but by the spring of 1321 the English still refused to recognise the independence of Scotland, and talks were abandoned. The English convinced the Pope that this breakdown was entirely the fault of the Scots, and in February 1321 he issued six papal bulls demanding that the Scottish bishops should appear before him, and that all invaders of England should be excommunicated.

In 1320, Bruce survived the biggest political crisis of his reign, when a conspiracy on his life was revealed. A group of former Balliol supporters, some of them signatories of the Declaration of Arbroath, conspired to place William Soulis on the throne. But the plot was revealed, and the conspirators tried for treason. Soulis was imprisoned, while others were executed.

Once again civil war threatened in England, over the King's new favourite, Hugh Despenser. He was opposed by Humphrey de Bohun, Earl of Hereford, and the Marcher Lords. The Earl of Lancaster sought Scottish assistance to dethrone Edward II. Lancaster conducted secret negotiations with Douglas and Randolph, but Bruce did not take these seriously.

When the two-year truce ended on 1 January 1322, Randolph, Douglas and Walter Stewart led renewed raids into England. The northern knights were defenceless without Lancaster's help, who *feigned excuse*. Edward II's main concern was to deal with the earls who opposed him. Lancaster and Hereford joined forces at Burton-on-Trent, but the English King drove them back. The Earls retreated north looking to join up with the Scots, but were cut off at Boroughbridge by Andrew Harclay, Governor of Carlisle. In the ensuing battle, on 16 March, Hereford was killed and Lancaster captured, whereupon Edward II had him beheaded without trial, revenge for the death of Piers Gaveston ten years before.

Now free of his domestic enemies, Edward II was confident that he could break the Scots by force. At Newcastle he assembled an army bigger than the one he had taken to Bannockburn, and had ships attack the west coast while others brought provisions to the Firth of Forth. On 1

July, while the English army assembled in the east, Bruce invaded England down the west coast, plundering through Cumberland and down to Lancaster and Preston. On his return to Scotland he camped near Carlisle for five days, using stolen cattle to trample and destroy the surrounding crops, before crossing the Border on 24 July.

Early in August the English army marched into Scotland. The main Scottish army was assembled to the north of the Forth. Bruce had evacuated all the land to the Border, clearing it of people and animals, and burning all crops and dwellings. Edward II marched to Edinburgh through a desolate land, and waited there for his provision ships, but they were delayed by adverse weather. Men were sent into the countryside to forage for food, finding nothing but a lame cow – the Earl of Surrey is said to have remarked: *This is the dearest beef that I ever saw; surely it has cost a thousand pounds or more!* By late September starvation forced the English army to withdraw.

Bruce, now with an enormous army at his disposal, invaded England again in the west, crossing the Solway on 1 October. His route took him to Northallerton where, on 12 October, he learned that the English King and Queen were at Rievaulx Abbey, 15 miles away. In an attempt to surprise them, Bruce made a forced march through the night, but in the morning he found his direct route blocked near Old Byland by a large force under the Earl of Richmond, overlooking a steep and rocky hillside. The only other route to Rievaulx was a 14-mile detour by Helmsley, but if they went that way Edward would have time to escape. Bruce chose to mount a frontal assault on the only narrow path

Rievaulx Abbey

up the hillside, defended by the enemy advance guard.

Douglas and Randolph led the attack, but when their progress was slow, Bruce ordered Highlanders to climb the cliffs to one side of the path and attack the English on their flank. When they reached the top, the Highlanders charged and – assaulted on two fronts – Richmond's force fell back, then fled. Richmond and many knights were captured, but Edward II had received warning and escaped. He fled to York, for the second time abandoning his baggage and treasure. The Earl of Richmond, a friend of the English King, was imprisoned for two years until his £20 000 ransom was paid. A number of French knights had been captured, including Henry de Sully, Grand Butler of France, but Bruce ensured that they were treated with hospitality and returned without ransom: Henry de Sully later acted as a liaison during truce negotiations. On 2 November the Scots returned home.

On 3 January 1323, Bruce was approached secretly by Andrew Harclay, now Earl of Carlisle. In the wake of the English King's failure to defend his people or to come to peace with the Scots, Harclay negotiated a peace on his own initiative. The treaty signed between himself and Bruce allowed for both countries to be independent, each with their own king and laws. Harclay returned to Carlisle and let the details of the treaty be known, but Edward II was outraged by this *treason*. Harclay was captured and tried on 2 March 1323, then hanged, disembowelled, beheaded and quartered.

Despite Harclay's execution, his proposals were popular, and on 30 May the English signed a 13-year truce which Bruce ratified eight days later. The English agreed not to oppose Scottish attempts to have the Papal interdict lifted, or to attack Scottish trading ships.

On New Year's Day 1324, Thomas Randolph, accompanied by Henry de Sully, received an audience with the Pope at Avignon. Randolph appealed to the Pope, explaining that Bruce was prevented from redeeming himself and joining a crusade by a clerical error: the omission of his title from Papal communications. Once Randolph's appeal had been expressed in such language, the Pope was happy to rectify this difficulty, and finally recognised Robert Bruce as King of Scots. Before long, however, he was further intimidated by Edward II to deny absolution until Berwick was returned to the English. The Scots refused.

Two months later, on 5 March, Queen Elizabeth gave birth to a son, David. At last Bruce had an heir. Edward II responded in July by bringing to his court Edward Balliol, the son and heir of King John. In November negotiations at York for a lasting peace failed, but hostilities were not resumed. In 1325 Bruce started building a manor house for his family at Cardross, near Dumbarton, overlooking the Clyde; and in the years of peace until 1327, he took care of political and economic matters at home. Early in 1326, King Robert's second son John died in infancy, and his lieutenant and son-in-law Walter Stewart also died. At a parliament at Cambuskenneth Abbey on 15 July, the succession to the Scottish throne was designated to Bruce's son David before Robert Stewart.

Relations between England and France had deteriorated, and in March 1325 Queen Isabella and her son, the Prince of Wales, had travelled to France to negotiate with her brother, Charles IV. But instead she received support from him to mount an invasion of England, and Bruce saw the opportunity to make a defensive alliance with France. Following negotiations led by Thomas Randolph, the Treaty of Corbeil was signed in April 1326.

Queen Isabella and her lover, Sir Roger Mortimer, sailed to England unopposed in September and made for London, supported by the Earls of Norfolk and Leicester. Edward II and Hugh Despenser tried to flee to Ireland, but were captured at Glamorgan in November. The King's favourite was executed, and Edward II was imprisoned in Kenilworth Castle, where he was forced to abdicate. On 1 February 1327 his son was crowned Edward III.

Bruce's nephew Donald, Earl of Mar, a lifelong friend of Edward II, sought help from Bruce to free the imprisoned King. Edward II escaped from Berkley Castle, but was soon recaptured, and Isabella decided he must be killed. He was starved and ill-treated, but did not die until his captors thrust a marrow bone into his rectum, and through it plunged a red-hot poker. On 21 September he was declared dead, and his outwardly unmarked body was displayed for public scrutiny.

11–A Final Victory

On the day of Edward III's coronation the Scots – freed from truce by Edward II's abdication – attacked Norham Castle. The truce was hastily renewed by the English, but Isabella and Mortimer, acting as Regents for the young English King, were already assembling a vast army at York. Bruce sailed to Ulster, and forced the English there to sign a one-year truce, rendering them inactive. Meanwhile Douglas, Randolph and Donald, Earl of Mar, led a raiding party over the Border and down to Weardale. On 10 July the enormous English army set out slowly for Durham, arriving on 18 July. They could see smoke from fires, and abandoning their baggage train they made a forced march to Haydon Bridge on the Tyne, where they expected the Scots to attempt a crossing.

In torrential rain, the Scots eluded them for two weeks until an English scout was captured and brought before Douglas, who allowed him to return to the English army with the details of the whereabouts of the Scots. In the morning the English marched to the Scottish position at the River Wear, finding the raiders drawn up on a hill on the other side. The river was too high after the rains to cross, and to the English request to fight on more open ground, the Scots replied, *We are here in your kingdom and have burnt and wasted your country. If you do not like it then come and dislodge us for we shall remain here as long as we please.* On 3 August, after some days of minor skirmishes, the Scots decamped under cover of night, withdrawing to a stronger position across the river at Stanhope Park. The following night Douglas led a raid on the English camp, and almost succeeded in an attack on the young King's tent.

On the night of the 5th, the English army stood to arms, awaiting another attack. But in the dark the Scots left camp fires clearly burning and crept away from Stanhope Park. By morning they were well on their way home. When the English King learned of the abject failure of his expedition, he burst into tears of rage. The weary and half-starved English army returned to York, and was disbanded.

With Ireland neutralised and the English in a pitiful state, Bruce led a fresh army into England in early September. He surrounded Norham and Alnwick, and proclaimed everywhere that he intended to annex the northern counties. Edward III could not fund another war - - and did not wish to lose part of his country – so two English envoys were sent to Norham to negotiate a lasting peace.

In October Bruce sent details of his six terms for peace: Robert I and his heirs were to have the kingdom free of any homage; his son David was to marry Edward III's sister Joan; no one in Scotland could hold lands in England, and vice versa; the two countries would have a military alliance, not affecting the Scottish alliance with France; Robert I would pay Edward III £20 000 within three years; Edward III would use his influence to have the Papal sentence of excommunication lifted. These proposals were very similar to those negotiated by Bruce and Andrew Harclay in 1323.

Still unable to accept his humiliation, Edward III wrote that he could only accept the marriage and the £20 000, but faced with little option he soon backed down and agreed to all of Bruce's terms. On 1 March 1328, at a parliament at York, letters to that effect were endorsed and given to the Scottish representatives, who took them to Edinburgh. On 17 March, in a chamber of Holyrood where King Robert lay ill, the final treaty documents were sealed and ratified. Present were a great many nobles and churchmen, among them Douglas and Randolph, and Bishop Lamberton, who died later that year.

As soon as the Treaty of Edinburgh was concluded, plans were made for the wedding between Bruce's four-year-old son David and Edward III's six-year-old sister Joan. The children were married on 12 July at Berwick, but neither king attended: Edward III declined, and Bruce excused himself through illness. Within weeks, however, Bruce went on

Whithorn Priory (see next page)

his final military expedition, when he accompanied William de Burgh, grandson of his deceased father-in-law, to Ulster. de Burgh was heir to the Red Earl, and Bruce's show of strength helped secure his heritage.

On his return, Bruce retired to his manor house at Cardross, staying there until February 1329. His illness grew steadily worse: it has been suggested that he suffered from leprosy, but this is unlikely as he was regularly allowed contact with friends and family until his death. In October 1328, the Pope finally lifted the sentence of excommunication from the King, but Bruce was a deeply pious man and he sought further absolution for his crimes. In February 1329 he left Cardross and made a very slow and laboured pilgrimage to St Ninian's Shrine at Whithorn, in southern Galloway. He spent several days there, fasting and praying.

He returned to Cardross in late April and, knowing his death to be imminent, summoned the leading noblemen of Scotland to his bedside, asking them to pledge their loyalty to his son. As Bruce had been unable in life to go on crusade, he asked instead that they choose one of themselves to take his heart to the Holy Land. They selected Sir James Douglas, and both Bruce and Douglas welcomed the choice.

A few days later on 7 June 1329, Robert Bruce, King of Scots, died. His heart was given to Sir James Douglas, and his body carried in a great procession to Dunfermline Abbey. He was buried in the choir of the abbey, near his Queen, Elizabeth – who had died two years earlier on 26 October 1327 – and among the former kings of Scots.

Douglas carried Bruce's heart in a silver casket on a

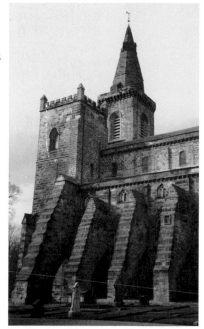

Dunfermline Abbey

The early 19th-century brass marking Bruce's tomb in Dunfermline Abbey. The Latin text reads: The tomb of Robert the Bruce, discovered by chance among the ruins in 1818, marked afresh by this brass in the 560th year after his death.

hain about his neck. Early in 1330 he sailed with six knights from Berwick to Flanders, and then to Spain, landing at Seville. He was welcomed there by Alfonso XI, King of Castile and Leon. When the Moorish King of Granada attacked Seville, Douglas's host asked him to lead the vanguard of his forces. Battle commenced on 25 March, but

Melrose Abbey – the heart of Robert the Bruce is buried here.

Douglas and a small group became separated and surrounded by Moors. Douglas and some of his knights were killed.

The heart of Bruce and the bones of Douglas were brought back to Scotland and buried: Bruce's heart at Melrose Abbey, and Douglas's remains at the Kirk of Douglas.

By 1332 Bruce's last great lieutenant, Thomas Randolph, Earl of Moray, was also dead. Warfare between England and Scotland soon began again – lasting intermittently for the next 400 years – but never again was Scotland in danger of becoming a nation subject to another. Robert Bruce had delivered his people from the aggressions of one of the most warlike nations in Europe, cementing once and for all the identity of a kingdom of Scots.

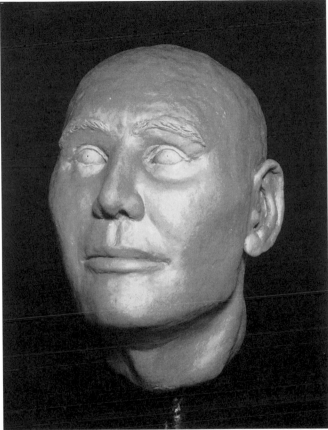

The reconstructed head of Robert the Bruce, built around a cast of his skull from his tomb at Dunfermline.

Map 5: Places to Visit in Scotland

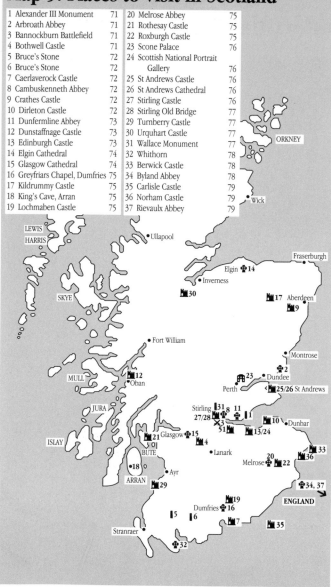

Places to Visit in Scotland

P	Parking
S	Sales Area
▆	Refreshments
WC	Toilet
£	Admission Charge
♿	Disabled
HS	Historic Scotland
NTS	National Trust for Scot.
EH	English Heritage

1 Alexander III Monument

NT 254864 66

On A921, E of Kinghorn, Fife

This monument, standing on King's Crag, marks the spot where Alexander III of Scotland fell from his horse and was killed on the night of March 18, 1286.

Open all year

2 Arbroath Abbey

NO 643413 54 HS

Off A92, in Arbroath, Angus

In 1320 the famous Declaration of Arbroath, asserting Scotland's independence from English rule, was written here, probably by Bernard Linton, Chancellor of Scotland and Abbot of Arbroath. Impressive portions of the abbey church remain. The abbot's house has been restored as a museum.

☎ 01241 878756—Open all year

P Nearby S £

3 Bannockburn Battlefield

NS 814917 57 NTS

Off M80/M9 at Junc 9, Bannock-burn, 2 miles S of Stirling

Standing on the site of the Battle of Bannockburn. Exhibits and audio-visual displays tell the story of Robert Bruce's greatest victory over the English. Nearby is the Rotunda, and the famous equestrian statue of the King – opened in 1964 – situated where Bruce himself stood on the first day of the battle.

☎ 01786 812664—Battlefield open all year; heritage centre open March to 23 December

P S WC £ ♿ Facilities

4 Bothwell Castle

NS 688594 64 HS

Off B7071, 1 mile S of Uddingston, Lanarkshire

One of the finest early castles in Scotland, it was besieged many times in the Wars of Independence. It was here that some 50 English nobles

Bothwell Castle

sought refuge after Bannockburn. Unfortunately, the castle warden changed sides when he heard of the Scottish victory and took them all prisoner.

☎ 01698 816894—Open all year except closed Thur PM and Fri in October to March

5 Bruce's Stone

NX 423798   77

Off A714, S side of Loch Trool, Dumfries & Galloway

An inscribed granite boulder commemorating Bruce's victory over the English here in April 1307.

Open all year – involves two mile walk

6 Bruce's Stone

NX 553768   77

By foot off A712, 6 miles W of New Galloway, Dumfries & Galloway

Another inscribed granite boulder on Moss Raploch, commemorating a victory there over the English in March 1307. This is probably a confusion with Loch Trool in April 1307.

Open all year – short walk

7 Caerlaverock Castle

NY 026656   84   HS

Off B725, 7 miles SE of Dumfries, Dumfries

One of the finest castles anywhere in Scotland. In 1300, Edward I's 3000-strong army took two days to capture it from only 60 defenders, a deed commemorated in the medieval French poem *Le Siege de Karlaverok*.

It was finally recaptured by the Scots in 1313.

☎ 01387 770244—Open all year

8 Cambuskenneth Abbey

NS 809939   57   HS

Off A907, Cambuskenneth, 1 mile E of Stirling

Cambuskenneth Abbey, now very ruinous, played an important part in the struggle for independence. Here in 1304 Bruce and Bishop Lamberton signed a bond of mutual assistance. The Abbey was also the scene of important Parliaments, especially in 1326.

View from exterior

9 Crathes Castle

NO 734968   45   NTS

Off A93, 3 miles E of Banchory, Aberdeenshire

A massive 16th-century tower house, built by the Burnetts, Crathes Castle has among its other attractions the jewelled ivory *Horn of Leys*, given to the Burnetts by Bruce in 1323.

☎ 01330 844525—Open April to October; grounds and gardens open all year

/Castle ground floor

10 Dirleton Castle

NT 518840   66   HS

Off A198, Dirleton, 2 miles W of North Berwick, Lothian

Dirleton Castle fell to Edward I's invading army in 1298 after a hard siege, shortly before the Battle of Falkirk. It was eventually recaptured and partly demolished by the Scots in

Dirleton Castle

1311. The castle was rebuilt, but is now a ruin.

Garden. Exhibition.

☎ 01620 850330—Open all year

11 Dunfermline Abbey

NT 089873 65 HS

Off A907 or A823, in Dunfermline, Fife

After Iona, Dunfermline became the traditional burial place of the Scottish Kings. The Abbey was ruined during the Reformation, although part of the church continued to be used. Bruce's tomb was rediscovered here in 1818 and is marked with a fine 19th century brass. Palace and ruins of domestic buildings.

Exhibition.

☎ 01383 739026—Choir of church closed October to March

P Nearby S &

12 Dunstaffnage Castle

NM 882344 49 HS

Off A85, 3.5 miles NE of Oban, Argyll

This imposing castle still retains its 13th century curtain wall. Bruce captured it from the MacDougall Lords of Lorne after his victory at the Pass of Brander in 1308, making it a royal possession with the Campbells as keepers.

☎ 01631 562465—Open April to September

P ☕ S WC & & WC

13 Edinburgh Castle

NT 252735 66 HS

Edinburgh

One of the strongest and most important castles in Scotland, Edinburgh Castle was recaptured for the Scots in 1314 by Thomas Randolph and his men after a daring night-time climb up the face of the rock.

The Stone of Destiny is displayed in the castle along with the Scottish Crown Jewels, as is the huge 15th-century cannon, Mons Meg. St Margaret's Chapel, dedicated to Queen Margaret, wife of Malcolm Canmore and built by her son David I, dates from the 12th century.

☎ 0131 225 9846—Open all year; courtesy vehicle can take visitors with disabilities to Crown Square

🅿 ☕ Ⓢ wc ♿

♿ wc/Facilities

14 Elgin Cathedral
NJ 222632 28 HS
Off A96, Elgin, Moray
The *Lantern of the North*, Elgin Cathedral – once one of the finest churches in Scotland – is now in ruins. Edward I visited here on his triumphant march around Scotland in 1296,

and again in 1303. The nearby castle was retaken by the Scots in 1308 and destroyed.

Exhibition.

☎ 01343 547171—Open all year – joint entry ticket with Spynie Palace

🅿 Nearby Ⓢ ♿

15 Glasgow Cathedral
NS 602655 64 HS
Centre of Glasgow
This Cathedral survived the Reformation intact, and is still the Parish Church of Glasgow. Robert Wishart, Bishop of Glasgow, was a prominent supporter of Bruce and Scottish independence. Much of the building dates from his time, between 1271 and 1316.

☎ 0141 552 6891—Open all year

☕ Ⓢ wc ♿ Access

Elgin Cathedral

16 Greyfriars Chapel, Dumfries

NX 971763 84

On A701, Dumfries

A modern church built in the grounds of the Franciscan friary where, in 1306, Robert Bruce murdered John Comyn. A plaque on a nearby building commemorates the event.

Site only

P Nearby

17 Kildrummy Castle

NJ 454164 37 HS

Off A97, 1 mile SW of Kildrummy village, Aberdeenshire

Although now ruinous, Kildrummy Castle was once one of the most powerful in Scotland. In 1306 Nigel Bruce was captured here when the castle was betrayed to the English after a hard siege. Nigel was taken to Berwick and executed.

✆ 01975 571331—Open April to September

P **S** **WC** £ **&** **WC**

18 King's Cave, Arran

NR 885310 69

Off A841, 2 miles N of Blackwaterfoot, Arran

This is reputedly where Bruce took refuge in his darkest hour. According to legend, he was about to abandon the unequal struggle against the English but, witnessing the efforts of a spider spinning its web, was inspired by its eventual success and vowed to continue his fight.

Open all year – two mile walk

19 Lochmaben Castle

NY 088812 78 HS

Off B7020, 0.5 miles S of Lochmaben, Dumfriesshire

The ruins of a later medieval castle, standing near the site of one of the hereditary strongholds of the Bruces, which saw many actions in the Wars of Independence.

Open all year – view from exterior

P

20 Melrose Abbey

NT 548341 73 HS

Off A6091, Melrose, Borders

This fine and substantial ruin is the burial place of Robert Bruce's heart. Excavations in September 1996 uncovered a leaden container, almost certainly holding the King's heart. It has since been reburied in the Abbey, and the spot marked.

✆ 01896 822562—Open all year

P **S** **WC** £

21 Rothesay Castle

NS 086646 63 HS

Off A844, in Rothesay, Bute

Surrounded by a wet moat and dating from the 12th century, this was one of the first castles Bruce seized in his uprising of 1306.

✆ 01700 502691—Open all year except closed Thurs PM and Fri October to March

P Nearby **S** £

22 Roxburgh Castle

NT 713337 74

Off A699, 1 mile W of Kelso, Borders

Little remains of what was one of the most powerful castles in Scotland. In

1314, Douglas recaptured it from the English by disguising himself and 60 followers as cattle – it was at nightfall – allowing them to approach and scale the wall undetected while the garrison feasted.

23 Scone Palace
NO 115267 58
Off A93, 2 miles N of Perth
The nearby Moot Hill was the ancient site of the inaugurations of the Kings of Scots, and the abbey the site of many parliaments – the Palace incorporates part of the Abbey buildings. Robert Bruce was crowned here in 1306. A replica of the Stone of Destiny, stolen by Edward I in 1296, is on display.

Scone Palace mostly dates from 1804, and is home to the Earls of Mansfield. Collections of furniture, clocks and porcelain. Gardens.

☎ 01738 552300—Open mid-April to October

🅿 ☕ Ⓢ 🚾 &

♿ 🚾/Facilities

24 Scottish National Portrait Gallery
NT 255743 66
Queen Street, Edinburgh
The Gallery has a bronze cast of the skull of Robert Bruce. In September 1996 a reconstruction of Bruce's face was made using forensic techniques, and this forms part of a larger display on the Kings and Queens of Scots. Also worth seeing is the mural of the Battle of Bannockburn.

☎ 0131 556 8921—Open all year

except Christmas and New Year

🅿 Nearby ☕ Ⓢ 🚾

♿ Facilities

25 St Andrews Castle
NO 513169 59 HS
Off A91, St Andrews, Fife
Close to the Cathedral. The Parliament of 1309 – the first free parliament in Scotland for eighteen years – was held here. Bruce was confirmed in his kingship by two declarations of support by the Scottish clergy and nobility.

Visitor centre. Exhibition.

☎ 01334 477196—Open all year; combined ticket available for castle and cathedral

🅿 Nearby Ⓢ 🚾 & ♿ 🚾

26 St Andrews Cathedral
NO 516166 59 HS
Off A91, St Andrews, Fife
Once the largest church in Scotland but now ruined, St Andrews Cathedral was consecrated in 1318. Robert Bruce attended the ceremony.

Museum houses a fine collection of early Christian and medieval sculpture.

☎ 01334 472563—Open all year; combined ticket available for cathedral and castle

🅿 Nearby Ⓢ &

27 Stirling Castle
NS 790940 57 HS
Stirling
Captured by the English in 1304 after a three-month siege, Edward I refused to let the defenders surrender until after he had tested his new siege-engine *War-Wolf* on them for a day.

Edward Bruce's failure to recapture it in 1313 became the trigger for Bannockburn.

Visitor centre. Exhibition. Garden.

☎ 01786 450000—Open all year

[P] [☕] [S] [WC] [♿]

[♿] [WC]/Access

28 Stirling Old Bridge

NS 797945   57

Off A9, N of Stirling Castle, Stirling

Although this bridge was built in the

Stirling Old Bridge

early 15th century, it stands on or very near the site of Wallace's crushing victory of Stirling Bridge in 1297. The road leading north from the bridge is still called *Causewayhead Road*. Part of the bridge was blown up in 1746 during the Jacobite Rising.

Open all year

29 Turnberry Castle

NS 196073   70

Off A77 and A719, 7 miles W of Maybole, Ayrshire

Very little remains of what once was a major Bruce stronghold and birthplace of King Robert I. Bruce landed at

Turnberry Point on his return to the mainland in 1307.

View from exterior

[P] Nearby

30 Urquhart Castle

NH 531286   26 HS

Off A82, 1.5 miles SE of Drumnadrochit, Highland

Standing in a picturesque location on the bank of Loch Ness, Urquhart Castle was captured and destroyed by Robert the Bruce in 1307 on his way towards Buchan. The fortress was rebuilt, but was dismantled in 1691 to prevent it being used by Jacobites. Impressive ruins remain.

01456 450551—Open all year

[P] [S] [WC] [♿]

31 Wallace Monument

NS 808956   57

Off B998, 1 mile NE of Stirling Castle

This famous monument to William Wallace stands on the Abbey Craig, where Wallace, Murray and their men positioned themselves before the Battle of Stirling Bridge in 1297. A

display includes Wallace's huge two-handed broadsword. There is a steep climb of 246 steps up to the monument.
☎ 01786 472140—Open March to October daily; February & November weekends only

P 🚐 S WC ⅋
♿ WC/Limited access

32 Whithorn Priory
NX 444403 83 HS
On A746 in Whithorn, Dumfries & Galloway
Robert the Bruce came on a pilgrimmage to Whithorn in 1329, shortly before his death. Substantial remains of the 12th-century church of a 12th-century priory, built on the site of community of St Ninian. Fine collection of early Christian sculpture. Visitor centre.
01988 500508—Open March to October

P Nearby ⅋

Places to Visit in England

33 Berwick Castle
NT 994535 75 EH
Adjacent to Berwick Railway Station, W of town centre
Once the greatest trading port in Scotland, Berwick changed hands several times throughout the Wars of Independence and was of extreme strategic importance. Now just inside the

English Border, much of the Elizabethan fortifications remain.
It was here that the *Ragman Roll* was signed in 1296, a list of Scottish property owners who swore allegiance to Edward I of England.
Open all year

34 Byland Abbey
SE 549789 100 EH
Off A170 at Coxwold, between Thirsk and Helmsley
Imposing ruins of a Cistercian abbey, near to the site of a battle where in 1322 the Scots defeated the English under the Earl of Richmond in an attempt to capture Edward II at Rievaulx Abbey.
☎ 01347 686614—Open all year

P S WC ⅋ ♿ WC/Access

Norham Castle (see next page)

Rievaulx Abbey

35 Carlisle Castle
NY 397563   85   EH
N of Carlisle town, Cumbria
An immense fortification in the north-west of England. The scene of many Anglo-Scottish confrontations throughout its history, it was besieged several times but never fell.
☎ 01228 591922—Open all year except Christmas and New Year
🅿 Nearby Ⓢ wc ⅃

36 Norham Castle
NT 907476   75   EH
Off B6470, 6 miles SW of Berwick-upon-Tweed
On a promontory in a curve of the River Tweed, this was one of the strongest of the Border castles.
☎ 0191 261 1585—Open all year
🅿 ☕ Ⓢ wc ⅃
♿ wc/Access excl keep

37 Rievaulx Abbey
SE 577489   100   EH
Off B1257, 2 miles W of Helmsley, Yorkshire
Impressive ruins of a Cistercian abbey. Edward II fled from here in 1322 at the approach of a Scottish force, leaving behind his personal goods and treasure to be captured by the Scots.
☎ 01439 798340—Open all year
🅿 ☕ Ⓢ wc ⅃ ♿ Facilities

79

Appendix I
Declaration of Arbroath, 1320

To the most Holy Father, the Lord John, by Divine Providence Supreme Pontiff of the Holy Roman and Universal Church, his humble and pious sons Duncan, Earl of Fife, Thomas Randolph, Earl of Moray, Lord of Man and of Annandale, Patrick Dunbar, Earl of March, Malise, Earl of Strathearn, Malcolm, Earl of Lennox, William, Earl of Ross, Magnus, Earl of Caithness and Orkney, and William, Earl of Sutherland; Walter, Steward of Scotland, William Soulis, Butler of Scotland, James, Lord of Douglas, Roger Mowbray, David, Lord of Brechin, David Graham, Ingram Umfraville, John Menteith, Guardian of the Earldom of Menteith, Alexander Fraser, Gilbert Hay, Constable of Scotland, Robert Keith,

Marischal of Scotland, Henry Sinclair, John Graham, David Lindsay, William Oliphant, Patrick Graham, John Fenton, William Abernethy, David Wemyss, William Mushet, Fergus of Ardrossan, Eustace Maxwell, William Ramsay, William Mowat, Alan Murray, Donald Campbell, John Cameron, Reginald Cheyne, Alexander Seton, Andrew Leslie, and Alexander Straiton, and the other barons and freeholders and the whole community of the realm of Scotland send all manner of filial reverence, with devout kisses of his blessed feet.

Most Holy Father and Lord, we know and from the chronicles and books of the Ancients we find that among other famous nations our own, the Scots, has been graced with widespread renown. They journeyed from Greater Scythia by way of the Tyrrhenian Sea and the Pillars of Hercules, and dwelt for a long course of time in Spain among the most savage tribes, but nowhere could they be subdued by any race, however barbarous. Thence they came, twelve hundred years after the people of Israel crossed the Red Sea, to their home in the west where they still live today. The Britons they first drove out, the Picts they utterly destroyed, and, even though very often assailed by the Norwegians, the Danes and the English, they took possession of that home with many victories and untold efforts; and, as the historians of old time bear witness, they have held it free of all bondage ever since. In their kingdom there have reigned one hundred and thirteen kings of their own royal stock, the line unbroken by a single foreigner.

The high qualities and deserts of these people, were they not otherwise manifest, gain glory enough from this: that the King of kings and Lord of lords, our Lord Jesus Christ, after His Passion and Resurrection, called them, even though settled in the uttermost parts of the Earth, almost the first to His most holy faith. Nor would He have them confirmed in that faith by merely anyone but by the first of His Apostles – by calling, though second or third in rank – the most gentle Saint Andrew, the Blessed Peter's brother, and desired him to keep them under his protection as their patron for ever.

The Most Holy Fathers your predecessors gave careful heed to these things and bestowed many favours and numerous privileges on this same kingdom and people, as being the special charge of the Blessed Peter's brother. Thus our nation under their protection did indeed live in freedom and peace up to that time when that mighty prince the King of the English, Edward, the father of the one who reigns today, when our kingdom had no head and our people harboured no malice or treachery and were then unused to wars or invasions, came in the guise of a friend and ally to harass them as an enemy. The deeds of cruelty, massacre, violence, pillage, arson, imprisoning prelates, burning down monasteries, robbing and killing monks and nuns, and yet other outrages without number which he committed against our people, sparing neither age nor sex, religion nor rank, no one could describe nor fully imagine unless he had seen them with his own eyes.

But from these countless evils we have been set free, by the help of Him who though He afflicts yet heals and restores, by our most tireless Prince, King and Lord, the Lord Robert. He, that his people and his heritage might be delivered out of the hands of our enemies, met toil and fatigue, hunger and peril, like another Macabaeus or Joshua, and bore them cheerfully. Him, too, divine providence, his right of succession according to our laws and customs which we shall maintain to the death, and the due consent and assent of us all have made our Prince and King. To him, as to the man by whom salvation has been wrought unto our people, we are bound both by law and by his merits that our freedom may be still maintained, and by him, come what may, we mean to stand.

Yet if he should give up what he has begun, and agree to make us or our kingdom subject to the King of England or the English, we should exert ourselves at once to drive him out as our enemy and a subverter of his own rights and ours, and make some other man who was well able to defend us our King; for, as long as but a hundred of us remain alive, never will we on any conditions be brought under English rule. It is in truth not for glory, nor riches, nor honours that we are fighting, but for freedom – for that alone, which no honest man gives up but with life itself.

Therefore it is, Reverend Father and Lord, that we beseech your Holiness with our most earnest prayers and suppliant hearts, in as much as you will in your sincerity and goodness consider all this, that, since with Him whose vice-regent on Earth you are there is neither weighing nor distinction of Jew and Greek, Scotsman or Englishman, you will look with the eyes of a father on the troubles and privations brought by the English upon us and upon the Church of God. May it please you to admonish and exhort the King of the English, who ought to be satisfied with what belongs to him since England used once to be enough for seven kings or more, to leave us Scots in peace, who live in this poor little Scotland, beyond which there is no dwelling-place at all, and covet nothing but our own. We are sincerely willing to do anything for him, having regard to our condition, that we can, to win peace for ourselves.

This truly concerns you, Holy Father, since you see the savagery of the heathen raging against the Christians, as the sins of Christians have indeed deserved, and the frontiers of Christendom being pressed inward every day; and how much it will tarnish your Holiness's memory if (which God forbid) the Church suffers eclipse or scandal in any branch of it during your time, you must perceive. Then rouse the Christian Princes who for false reasons pretend that they cannot go to the Holy Land because of wars they have on hand with their neighbours. The real reason that prevents them is that in making war on their smaller neighbours they find quicker profit and weaker resistance. But how cheerfully our Lord the King and we too would go there if the King of the English would leave us in peace, He from whom nothing is hidden well knows; and we profess and declare it to you as the Vicar of Christ and to all Christendom.

But if your Holiness puts too much faith in the tales the English tell and will not give sincere belief to all this, nor refrain from favouring them to our prejudice, then the slaughter of bodies, the perdition of souls, and all the other misfortunes that will follow, inflicted by them on us and by us on them, will, we believe, be surely laid by the Most High to your charge.

To conclude, we are and shall ever be, as far as duty calls us, ready to do your will in all things, as obedient sons to you as His Vicar; and to Him as the Supreme King and Judge we commit the maintenance of our cause, casting our cares upon Him and firmly trusting that He will inspire us with courage and bring our enemies to nought.

May the Most High preserve you to His Holy Church in holiness and health and grant you length of days.

Given at the monastery of Arbroath in Scotland on the sixth day of the month of April in the year of grace thirteen hundred and twenty and the fifteenth year of the reign of our King aforesaid.

Appendix II: Good King Robert

Robert Bruce has been portrayed as many different things, from a patriotic hero to an aristocratic Norman adventurer with nothing but his own self-interest at heart. How, then, can these extreme points of view be reconciled?

The Norman French family of de Brus – from Brix, near Cherbourg – had acquired their Scottish lands from David I, King of Scots – who reigned from 1124 to 53 – encouraged many Norman families to come north of the Border. The de Brus lands were in Annandale, where they settled and intermarried with other noble Scottish and English families. King Robert was unquestionably Scottish; born and raised in the south-west of the country, he was the great-great-great grandson of the original de Brus of Annandale. He was also the great-great-great-great grandson of David I, King of Scots. To call him a Norman is surely taking genealogy too far.

On July 11, 1274, Robert Bruce was born into one of the most important families in Scotland, one which enjoyed close royal connections and which, after the death of the Maid of Norway in 1290, possessed a very real and powerful claim to the throne. Bruce was only 18 when his family's claim to the Scottish throne was rejected in favour of John Balliol. He was 22 when Edward I denied his family the throne on Balliol's abdication. Whatever the legal rights and wrongs of the case, this must have had a huge effect on him. Born in an age where blood and right went hand-in-hand, young Robert was powerfully aware of how close he stood to the Scottish throne. Kingship meant more than wealth and political power: it was a status granted by God, a divine right.

Bruce certainly changed sides in the early years of the Scottish resistance. Although as one of the leading magnates of Scotland he had acted as a Guardian, Bruce submitted to Edward I in 1302, some two years before the other leading Scottish nobles, including Comyn. Behind this was the threat in 1302 of the return of John Balliol, backed by a French army. The reinstatement of King John would place the Comyns in a supreme position in Scotland, and would result in the loss of all Bruce's Scottish lands. Robert Bruce wanted to see a kingdom of Scotland, free and independent of English domination, but he wanted to be at its head. He knew that Edward I was an old man, and that his son, Edward of Caernarvon, was not the warrior his father had been. But if King John was to be reinstated with French support, and Edward I was to die before he could defeat Balliol again, then the Scottish throne could fall irrevocably into the hands of the Comyn faction. Bruce's own right of Kingship would be forever lost.

Undoubtedly, this was a self-interested stance to take, far removed from the apparent patriotic heroism of Wallace. Many people, taken aback at this treachery from one of Scotland's national heroes, have rejected Bruce and with him many of the other noble families who swapped allegiances with the changing fortunes of war. William Wallace, however, can be drawn out as a paragon of patriotic virtue, a common man ever loyal to his native land, who never submitted to English tyranny. To heighten this impression, Bruce has been portrayed as merely a self-serving aristocrat, not Scottish at all but actually foreign and *Norman*. But to do this is to commit the greatest of mistakes in history: trying to judge the actions of the past by modern standards. To criticise Bruce for his lack of patriotism and national loyalty is like criticising Chaucer for his lack of feminist principles, or Edward I for his failure to create a fair and equal society. Patriotism and nationalism were alien concepts in Medieval Europe. Wallace, indeed, is a remarkable figure in this respect, although it is probably better to see him as a loyalist to Balliol and to the Scottish Crown as an abstraction, rather than to the nation of Scotland.

If Bruce had merely been a self-aggrandising brigand, would he have risked all his extensive English and Scottish estates in his desperate gamble in 1306? He made an implacable enemy not only of the English king but also of the powerful Comyn faction in Scotland. Bruce loved Scotland and believed he was her rightful king. King and Kingdom were indivisible; one could not exist without the other. The Kingdom of Scotland, with himself as King of Scots, was worth any risk.

Robert Bruce certainly had great courage, but as King his personal leadership in engagements such as the attack on Perth in 1313 or his duel with de Bohun could be regarded as foolish and foolhardy. But Bruce could not merely be a skilled general and warrior: he had to become, in the words of Professor Barrow, *a Joshua, a captain of his people.* He inspired great loyalty, and his generous and kingly nature was acclaimed even by English chroniclers of the time. In his younger days he had certainly been rash and impetuous, even violent – the murder of John Comyn of Badenoch, whether Bruce struck the fatal blow or not, still must cling to him – but, having learned patience in his years as a fugitive, he never forgot the lesson.

He also never forgot his friends, rewarding loyalty with loyalty, and he made every effort to reconcile his Scottish enemies, with the single exception of the Comyns. Never again would this family achieve anything approaching their previous status. The families of Campbell, Douglas, MacDonald and, of course, Stewart date their rise to power and prominence from this period.

Bruce had fought against England for almost half his life, and yet he desired only peace – and acknowledgement of his status as king of an equal and independent kingdom. Despite all the difficulties of the English crown through these years, despite their defeats and reversals, despite the hardship and suffering of the northern counties, Edward II refused to countenance such an agreement. It was not until Edward III came to power, 15 years old and new to his throne, that peace was possible. Even then this was at least partly due to Bruce's threat – however unlikely – to annex the northern counties and add them to Scotland.

At last, at the end of his life, Bruce had achieved what he had long fought for. Scotland was once again an independent kingdom. The legacy of

Statue of Robert the Bruce at Bannockburn

his struggle for freedom was a heavy one. Scotland had earned the implacable hostility of the English kings; raids and warfare had become a way of life in the Borders; for hundreds of years, Scotland and England would be enemies. And yet Scotland remembers him as *Good King Robert*, and his triumph at Bannockburn is a rallying cry to Scots everywhere. Although throughout the Middle Ages and beyond, Scotland would often be in peril from English aggression and invasion, it would never again be conquered. Bruce's final legacy was to confirm Scotland as separate and distinct, not just as a kingdom but as a community, a people and ultimately a nation.